A writer's first-hand account of 1980s Colombia

This is a nonfiction work. Although the accounts and places in Walking in the Clouds are real, some of the names have been changed to protect the privacy of certain individuals and the identity of others.

WALKING IN THE CLOUDS
Colombia through the eyes of a gringo

MICHAEL F. KASTRE

SAINT MICHAEL'S PRESS

Also by Michael F. Kastre

The Minority Career Guide
The Way We Were - The Baby Boomer Story

About the Author

Michael F. Kastre is a Washington, D.C.-based writer who has written over 500 articles and columns for numerous magazines, newspapers and online publications. He's covered a spectrum of topics ranging from politics, health, and technology to terrorism, business, and military affairs.

Michael traveled extensively in South America for several decades, working full-time in Colombia as a photojournalist for over 3 years. He also spent a number of years working as a consultant for various Department of Defense programs, including the Missile Defense Agency and the Airborne Warning and Control System (AWACS), and covered Capitol Hill for seven years as a military affairs correspondent. In addition, he served as an adjunct faculty member for several universities, teaching undergraduate courses in advanced research and writing, business, and communications.

Michael resides in the Potomac Highlands of West Virginia with his wife, Nydia, who is also a writer. When not at home writing or working on his garden, he enjoys traveling and visiting family throughout Italy, Morocco and Colombia.

You can contact him at michael@michaelkastre.com

For my wife Nydia—always my little flower, she inspires, personifies love and patience, and is the best partner a man could ever hope to have. She is the reason this work came to life with her gentle nudges and reminders that it was a journey and a story worth sharing. This book is also dedicated to our remarkable daughters, Natalie and Veronica, who bring love, joy, and perspective into our lives. In addition, I express my deepest appreciation to my equally remarkable sons-in-law, Craig and Hedeer, for their keen insight and suggestions on how to frame and capture events long past.

We all have our time machines—memories take us to our past and dreams transport us to our future. Of course, just like it is never good to fret too much about the future, it is never good to dwell too much in the past, but it does provide perspective and context to contemporary times. As some of yesterday's great writers and patriots have noted...

The past is never dead. It's not even past.
—WILLIAM FAULKNER

I know of no way of judging the future but by the past.
—PATRICK HENRY

If you want to understand today, you have to search yesterday.
—PEARL BUCK

The past, when combined with journeys and new destinations can be a life changing, soul wrenching experience as some prominent writers and thinkers have wisely noted...

Travel is fatal to prejudice, bigotry, and narrow-mindedness.
—MARK TWAIN

There are no foreign lands. It is the traveler only who is foreign.
—ROBERT LOUIS STEVENSON

A journey is like marriage. The certain way to be wrong is to think you control it.
—JOHN STEINBECK

One's destination is never a place, but a new way of seeing things.
—HENRY MILLER

All journeys have secret destinations of which the traveler is unaware.
—MARTIN BUBER

AUTHOR NOTES

The old adage that the truth is often stranger than fiction has much merit, as witnessed by this gringo's adventures in Colombia, a truly magical country inhabited by remarkable people. The places in Walking in the Clouds are real and the events actually happened. Many of the names have been altered to protect the privacy of some individuals and the identity of others—both the innocent and the guilty.

Although I continue to spend considerable time in Colombia, a couple of decades have passed since I lived and worked there as a freelance photojournalist. During that time much has changed, and yet, little has changed. The series of events set forth here, and my experiences covering them, occurred from 1984 to 1987. As appropriate, I have endeavored to put these into context by observations of current affairs and brief glimpses at historical events.

Life is truly uncharted territory, revealing its story one moment at a time. Looking back I realize now that my journey was not just a series of random moments in time, but rather a string of often unexpected occurrences. At times the impressions they made on me assaulted my senses and still linger in my mind. All of them shaped not only my time in Colombia, but they also impacted my subsequent life. To me, this is confirmation that the richness of life for all of us lies in the memories we have made.

The 1980s were before the rise of digital photography. Accordingly, many of the photographs I took during that era have suffered the ravages of time and faded. No matter, the images in my mind remain vivid. I must confess that with the passage of time, though, some have dimmed as well. Although not perfect, I have included a few of the images I captured during my time in Colombia.

In chronicling the stories, I have relied on my recollections, journal notes, and partially on information contained in stories I wrote at the time. Any errors in historical facts or places are unintended and such errors are mine, and mine alone.

I have also tried to put the stories in chronological order; however, since each story is a standalone vignette and may span a period of time, this was not always possible.

—Michael F. Kastre

Source: CIA Open Domain Information

TABLE OF CONTENTS

PREFACE

Walking in the Clouds—Colombia through the Eyes of a Gringo is based on what I saw and experienced while working in the country as a photojournalist. From the Torching of the Judicial Palace and Conversations with a Guerrilla to Carnival and a Water Tower view of the Pope, they provide a timeless lens through which to view not only Colombia, but Latin America as a whole. In many ways, the accounts also provide a mirror that reflects back a realistic perspective of how others see us.

Colombia represents not only the promise, but the problems that haunt an entire continent. The continent's gateway, Colombia is South America's oldest surviving democracy. Although its democracy is fragile at times it has proven extremely resilient, even in the current sea of political turmoil.

Even its geography reflects the contradiction that is Colombia. It is both united and divided by the lofty Andes Mountains. Given the mountains and its proximity to the equator, Colombia's seasons are all stacked on top of each other, creating literal layers of eternal spring, summer, and fall, depending on the elevation. Bogota, for example, is a land of forever autumn while the city of Medellin enjoys a spring-like climate year round.

Its past and future are tantalizing. Colombia was the centerpiece of Simon Bolivar's dream of a united South America that never materialized. Nonetheless, Colombia combines the splendor of colonial Spain with the energy of modern Latin America. Its politics are volatile and often plagued by dangerous alliances between violent leftist guerrilla groups and powerful drug cartels.

Despite the fame of Colombian coffee and its notoriety for drugs, however, most people know little about the country. As colored through its stories, Walking in the Clouds—Colombia through the Eyes of a Gringo provides a look at Colombian history, politics, psyche, culture, and contradictions. It begins with a glimpse of Colombia's essence and the source of many of its underlying beliefs and fundamental challenges. They are what not only shaped 1980s Colombia, but what continue to impact it today.

The Soul & Psyche of Colombia

The coast is the beat that forms the rhythm of Colombia, but the soul of the country is the Andes.

Lofty, often shrouded in clouds, these majestic mountains offer spectacular and haunting vistas. It's as though the hardy souls who trekked the countless crests and lived for millennia in the high valleys of the Andes still drift through its mist and float on the wisps of clouds. The coast provides balance with its steamy, colorful lowlands crowned with palms and lush tropical vegetation. Its energy pulses through both its people and landscape.

One thing, though, is common. That is, how they view the outside world. Colombians think we take them for granted. And, to a large measure they have compelling reasons to believe that; however, like other Latinos, they take this form of being a victim even further. Indeed, to some extent, the Latin American mentality colors most things that happen in Colombia, including the stories in this book. Cuba, for example, has been the model for revolution on the continent for decades. Colombia has not been immune from this romantic, yet false and destructive notion of rebellion as a means to address all social and economic inequities, as noted below in the excerpt of a story I filed at the time.

Sowing the Seeds for Chaos & the Latin American Myth[1]

As an integral part of Latin America, Colombia is part of a ten-thousand mile

---

1 Adapted from a column by Michael F. Kastre, which appeared in the Birmingham Post-Herald, January 7, 1987

tapestry that stretches from the U.S. border to the Antarctic. Although Colombia, like other Latin countries, is unique, it shares many common traits with its neighbors, including economic, social, and political challenges. But, the most striking common denominator is the tendency to blame any lack of development on US imperialism. This insidious myth pervades every corner of Latin America.

In 1959 the myth was strengthened, for a period of time, when Fidel Castro fought his way to power in Cuba. By turning his back on the United States and promising sweeping economic and social changes, many believed the Cuban leader would prove that once completely free from US influence, a Latin country could truly prosper.

In the early years, Cuba's revolution captured the imagination of many liberal thinkers, not only in Latin America, but around the world. This illusion, however, was short-lived. After decades of repression and hardship, the dismal failure of the Cuban revolution has diminished, but not destroyed, the intervention myth.

The root causes for chaos and the relative failure of Latin America and the unsurpassed success of the United States are found in history, not North American imperialism. It was the good fortune of the North Americans to be colonized by Britain. At the time, the English were endowed with Europe's highest levels of technology, economics, and political institutions.

The influence of the world's first industrialized nation was directly applied to the colonies, planting the entrepreneurial seed. Even after the American Revolution, the fever for development and expansion continued to be partially fueled by British influence.

To the south, it was Latin America's fate to be colonized by Spain. A country estimable in many ways, but nonetheless a country, which after its "golden century" in the 1500s, was in decline. The defeat of its armada by England in 1588, and continuous wars in Europe, slowly sapped the country's strength and lowered its world position.

Spain's industrial and scientific development lagged behind that of its neighbors. Their pre-capitalist system did little to stimulate innovation. In addition, Spanish political institutions did not develop along parliamentary lines, further inhibiting change. The Spanish New

World was a mirror of the old.

Although side by side in the same hemisphere, the seeds for the emergence of different systems had been sown. Those who settled the cornerstone of North America came looking for land, liberty, and an opportunity for prosperity.

In contrast, the Spanish conquistadors sought different riches. They were driven by the glittering legend of El Dorado, the mythical Lost City of Gold. It was never found and eventually life took on a more routine nature. Once the Spaniards took off their armor and settled down, they created a more corseted and rigid society than the one they had escaped in search of instant riches, fame, and adventure.

In time they yearned for independence, but were totally unprepared for it since they had no experience with a democratic style system. After cutting himself away from Spain, the Latino was left alone to figure out who he was. He was aware of the North American experiment, but unsure how to establish such a system for himself.

The great liberator, Simon Bolivar, had dreams of a united Latin America. A nation called Gran Colombia, comprised of present day Colombia, Venezuela, Ecuador, and part of Panama, was established for a short time around 1819, but fell apart barely ten years later because of bickering and factionalism. This was due in large part to a clinging to the old feudal ideas of hereditary power and landed gentry.

This legacy, inherited from Spain, kept the Latino from ever fully establishing a democracy. Instead, in the aftermath of the Latin revolution, power did not find its way to the people. It remained in the hands of a few, paving the way for the rich to keep control through the military.

Out of all this grew machismo, which even today still pervades how Latinos deal with each other and strangers. It also instilled a pervasive suspicion of outsiders. (Something I was destined to find out first-hand.)

Ironically, when Spain swept away 40 years of right-wing dictatorship in 1976 and laid the foundation for a surprising advance by the country into the modern European community, Colombia and other Latin countries did not automatically follow the example. With the exception of Colombia, today the continent seems headed in the opposite direction. This is surprising given the profound failure in Cuba, now most notably being repeated in Venezuela, Ecuador, and Bolivia where self-labeled socialist leaders seem determined to become dictators for life.

Latinos have for the most part silently tolerated Castro's tendency to try and export his failed revolution to their shores, while still vocally promoting and clinging to the myth that US intervention is responsible for their miseries and failures. Surprising since underneath the images, pretensions, and blunders are a people who long for liberty and a system that will present an opportunity for prosperity and stability.

They surely will not find such a system in communism or even hardcore socialism. Only by looking to the past and not reliving it, can they find their roots and adequate answers to the facts of history.

Colombia has a larger middle class than the majority of its neighbors. One which is broad based and well developed. I attribute this to its basic adherence to democracy and freedom even despite a tumultuous time known as the "Period of Violence" between 1948 and 1958, during which liberals and conservatives killed each other by the thousands. The political feud was sparked by the assassination of Jorge Eliecer Gaitan, a popular liberal leader.

To their credit, though, true democracy returned to Colombia in 1958 after the formation of a coalition government when moderate leftists and conservatives worked out a compromise. In the period that followed, the faltering economy stabilized and agrarian reform was instituted. Entire books have been written on this dangerous time. I mention it only to put things into context.

Unfortunately, a negative outcome of this time was the rise of several different leftist guerrilla groups. The two dominant rebel groups are the Revolutionary Armed Forces of Colombia—known by its Spanish acronym, FARC—and the National Liberation Army, called the ELN. The FARC, founded by the Colombian Communist Party, and ELN both came into existence in the 1960s after the Period of Violence. Of these, the FARC became the more dominant.

With the rise of powerful drug cartels in the 1980s, as Colombia became the primary source of the world's cocaine trade, these leftist revolutionaries started providing protection in the form of armed muscle to the drug lords in exchange for money to operate and buy arms. The result, under a series of Colombian presidents who attempted to appease or negotiate with them, has been continued violence and insecurity within the country with the rebels actually controlling large areas at times.

That all changed with the election of Alvaro

Uribe in 2002. From a shaky start during which his inauguration at Casa Nariño (the equivalent of our White House) underwent a mortar attack by guerrillas, Uribe ushered in a new era in Colombia and brought enormous changes to the country. During the ceremony two shells landed near the presidential palace and fourteen people were killed and forty wounded as he was sworn in as president.

During Uribe's tenure the drug gangs and the rebels suffered the loss of over half their combat strength. By 2009, the government had gained control of well over 95 percent of Colombian territory, as opposed to controlling only about 50 percent if it in 2002.

In addition, crime statistics changed dramatically. Murders declined by over 50 percent, kidnappings went down by 85 percent, and, many key leaders of both the drug cartels and rebel groups were captured or killed.

It's against this backdrop of history and current affairs that I recount my experiences related to a series of events, many of which continue to impact the country.

What I've Learned, In General

In the spirit of full disclosure, I tend to be highly skeptical and criticize people who speak in generalities. Things are usually more nuanced, more layered, or more complex than that. Yet, I find myself doing the same thing here. That is, in general, Latinos genuinely like North Americans as individuals, but they are distrustful of our international corporations and government. In general, not only do they tend to blame outsiders—including our government and corporations—for many of their woes, but they feel that they have been put upon and taken advantage of over the years.

In general, despite the fact that they distrust Uncle Sam and American international business enterprises, they have an underlying respect for the US and, indeed, many even want to resettle to the north.

In general, based on my experience and observations, I believe these factors are part of the contradiction and dichotomy of the Latin perspective and mentality, driving much of their seemingly inconsistent behavior.

In general, I learned that pride combined with machismo can create a lot of misunderstandings and misconceptions. Specifically, I learned that you can never overlook or dismiss pride—the very word which unfortunately often has a negative connotation. We sometimes even mistake it for arrogance, especially in Latinos because their pride includes an element of machismo. The truth is, of course, that people in all countries have national pride. Colombians are certainly no exception, voicing a strong pride in all aspects of their country from its natural beauty to their lifestyles and way they do things.

We North Americans become upset when others step on our pride. We should expect no less when others perceive that we do the same thing. We think our ways are the best and often fail to understand things that don't reflect our approach. We often verbalize this and it spills over to everything from culture and heritage to education and such unlikely things as driving and traffic. There is hardly an aspect of life in countries like Colombia that is immune from criticism or comment from outsiders.

Nonetheless, it's difficult not to have preconceived ideas and perspectives. I certainly had mine when I went south to live. Right or wrong, they were based on my personal beliefs and my life experiences. I still struggle not to judge or form opinions about others unless I have truly walked in their shoes.

By being a witness to events which characterized 1980s Colombia, I've learned to listen more closely to people and nature. For me they are elusive and at times difficult to grasp, but I believe that both have consistent rhythms. Just as North and South America are divided by such things as language and culture, there are also common emotions, dreams, hopes, fears, and frustrations that unite us. These threads are woven through the same human mosaic that should give us all a healthy measure of understanding and optimism about the future.

In general, based on that, I found that Colombians see too many gringos as predictable. Too often they think we sound like this: "Why do you do it that way... That's not the way we do it... If you don't like the way we do it, why did you come to this country?"

In general, in my travels, it bothered me to be painted

with the same broad brush. On reflection, though, I could see their point since we often do things through our behavior and words that to us may seem innocent, but which are perceived by others to be arrogant and insensitive. Not surprisingly, it colors relationships— whether between individuals or countries.

INTRODUCTION
WALKING IN THE CLOUDS—A GRINGO STARTS A NEW LIFE IN COLOMBIA

My wife is from Colombia, but we met and married in Washington, DC. In 1984, after a decade of marriage, we decided to take our two young daughters and move to Colombia. I was working as an engineer for a large consulting company, but freelance writing had been increasingly occupying my time.

Since I had a technical background, I had always found comfort in the certainty of science and numbers. This, though, was at odds with my planned journey because when I logically evaluated the tools and advantages I had at my disposal to carve out a new life, it didn't add neatly up. Accordingly, during those days, my mood alternated between uncertainty and confidence. On a gut level I thought I could make it, but on paper my chances didn't look so promising.

Nonetheless, I took the plunge. I submitted my letter of resignation and left my well-paying position for the uncertainty and excitement of full time freelance writing. I have never looked back.

After making arrangements to rent our house, a company came to pack our household goods—all 10,000 pounds—and had them shipped to Colombia. They were stored in a cargo container and placed on a ship. Weeks later they arrived at the Colombian seaport of Barranquilla. From there they were trucked to Bogota.

Our ultimate destination was Pasto in the department of Nariño—the equivalent of a state in the US. Colombia consists of 32 departments. Each has a capital city of at least 500 thousand population, with over 70 percent of the country's 45 million living in urban areas.

Pasto, a city of about half a million, is located in the southwest corner of the country. It was a city I had visited many times and had fallen in love with its location, rich history, and the beauty of the surrounding countryside.

But first we had to deal with customs in Bogota. At the time, they had very tight control on imports in an effort to reduce contraband and collect taxes. When we showed up with lots of furniture, a washer and dryer, a considerable collection of wine, and a host of small appliances, the customs officer informed us that we would have to pay import tax on the items. We politely informed him that we disagreed because we didn't want to sell the goods, but rather they were items for our personal use.

I refer to this initial time in Colombia as our "held

hostage in customs" period because it turned into a tug of war between us and the officials. This went on for almost three months as they refused to release our goods unless we paid the tax and us refusing to pay such a tariff. Our refusal was based partly on principle and partly on limited financial resources.

Typical Pasto street scene circa 1985.

Looking back, it probably could have all been settled early on if I had discretely paid some pesos under the table and parted with a few cases of wine. Not fully understanding the prevailing culture, though, I failed to capitalize on this method of breaking the impasse. For her part, my wife knew, but was even more firm in standing on principle. They must have thought we were either incredibly cheap or just naïve. Or perhaps they thought we were just arrogant. I will never know.

Finally, our war of wills ended when my wife found a lawyer in customs who agreed with us. A calm man of integrity, he was more than generous with his time trying to help us. Armed with a letter from his office we were able to prevail. At the warehouse, though, I didn't make any friends and the customs official we had been dealing with scowled the whole time our goods were being loaded onto a truck. At one point I heard him ask another official how we had managed to spring our goods without paying. The other man just shrugged. My nerves were taut and I didn't relax until our precious cargo was safely away from the official warehouse complex.

We used some of our limited funds to buy a white Fiat station wagon. It would turn out to be one of the best cars I ever owned. We packed the kids in and set off for Nariño.

That was just the beginning. Once we arrived in Pasto, we had to find a house to rent, which turned out to be no small feat. To be sure, there were plenty of them available, but the state of the local telecommunications at that time was such that if you didn't rent a house that had a telephone, you were not going to have one for the foreseeable future. This was, of course, well before such technological marvels as cell phones.

You also have to imagine a world without personal computers and the Internet. I wrote my stories on a portable manual Smith & Corona typewriter. Photocopy machines were hard to find and if you did find one, copies were expensive. When writing I used carbon paper. (When I tell my kids that, they think I'm joking.)

Sometimes I was able to fax my stories to the US, but mostly I relied on the mail service. On a few occasions, when my editors needed the story immediately, I would go to the commercial telecom office and pay for a long distance call and slowly read the story to an editor on the other end who would dutifully copy it down.

There were no ATMs so dealing with money was also a problem. This was one challenge, however, that I had anticipated before leaving the States. I addressed it by building a wine rack with a hidden door in the bottom, which provided access to a strong box. Cash was king, but dollars had to be turned into pesos at the Bank of the Republic—the government's national bank.

During our house hunting period, my brother-in-law Eudoro and sister-in-law Mary graciously let us stay with them. We finally found a suitable house with a telephone in a section of the city called "Palermo" on Calle 39 (39th street). This would later prove to be a life saver, but I am getting ahead of myself.

The house itself was splendid with its marble floors, fireplace, and indoor garden in the living room. It had a stately staircase that swept up in a curve from the foyer to the second story bedrooms. Best of all, though, was that we could walk the girls to the school where they were initially enrolled. We also had a real milkman who delivered raw milk in small metal milk cans to our doorstep in a horse drawn wagon. We would then put these on the stove to pasteurize.

At that time, there were only eight foreigners in the entire department. These included an Italian and a German, but most of the others were from Holland and engaged in manufacturing furniture from the region's plentiful supply of exotic wood. I was the only American gringo. The locals never stopped wondering what I was doing there. I would always explain that I was a writer and journalist. I would also explain how we wanted our girls to be in a small city where they would have the best opportunity to assimilate and appreciate the culture of their mother's country.

The question of the day, however, remained, "What is a gringo doing here?" The most rampant rumor was that I worked for the CIA or was some kind of other spy for the U.S. government. I found all of this a little humorous; although a bit unnerving since I have never worked for the US government, other than my stint in the military. No matter. Until the day I left, I was the gringo CIA man. (I must say, though, that the people were wonderful to me and my family and a joy to spend time with.) Finally, we settled in and I found myself living in the magical environment of which I had long dreamed.

As for how they referred to me, some may view the word "gringo" as derogatory in some way. I don't. Although born in Michigan, I grew up in Southern Arizona and it's something I had heard all my life.

With various competing thoughts on its origins there doesn't seem to be any real consensus about the term. I was taught that the word comes from the song called "Green Grow the Lilacs" sung by Americans during the Mexican-American War. After hearing this repeatedly, the Mexicans eventually changed "green grows" to "gringos" and took to calling the Americans by this name. I also heard that it came from the word *griego*, which is Spanish for Greek and sometimes applied as slang to any foreigner. I am not an expert on languages so I don't know if what I was told is accurate or there is another explanation. What I do know is that I personally never took offense to being called a gringo.

Walking in the Clouds

I have always been fascinated by the way the clouds caress the Andes. Pasto, where I made my home base, is well over 8,000 feet. Its elevation and proximity to the equator make it a land of forever fall. Dominated by the lofty Galeras Volcano, towering over 14,000 feet, the surrounding countryside is a patchwork of lush green and amber fields, picturesque pueblos, and small coffee farms. On a typical day there is brilliant sun in some parts of the deep blue sky. Other parts are marked with thick, dark clouds that billow by, driven by the wind. Since they nestle down on the land, when in the Andes, walking in the clouds is often literal. This characteristic of the country is one I love.

During my time in Colombia, walking in the clouds

also came to symbolize how my wife, with good humor I must add, claimed that I walked with my head in the clouds much of the time because of the somewhat less than sane adventures I often embarked upon and the less than savory characters I associated with.

Clouds settle over a typical landscape in Nariño

As I recount later in the book, while I was interviewing a Marxist guerrilla I asked him why they didn't try to change the system at the ballet box instead of with bullets. I have never forgotten his testy response. He said, "And you call me an idealist. What you say is pure gringo bullshit. Look, to understand you have to stop looking at us and our struggle through the eyes of a gringo."

At the time, though, I was undaunted and began to look for my first story. It didn't take long for it to find me.

1

FROM BANK ROBBER TO FAMOUS WRITER

Late Summer 1984

Perhaps it's fitting that I got my first "promotion" of sorts in an unusual way during my transition to a full time writer. It started on what promised to be a fun, but uneventful day.

La Cocha is one of the most beautiful spots in Colombia. Less than an hour drive from Pasto, the sparsely populated area has a high mountain lake teaming with trout. Over the years several families of German and Swiss ancestry have built lodges on its banks. These combination hotels and restaurants are popular places to visit, either for a leisurely lunch or dinner or to spend a few days.

From my early days of visiting Colombia, I was always captivated by the mysterious beauty of the area. Often covered by clouds and a lack of bright sunny days, it can have a somewhat dark presence, but not in a sinister sense. It's a place unlike any I have ever visited. One has the sense of a high alpine region, cold, yet made hospitable by its pristine blue waters and Swiss style inns with their roaring stone fireplaces, solid beams, and wood paneling.

My wife, Nydia, and I at La Cocha, 1985

During that time, my favorite place on the lake was a Bavarian inn, which sat on a rectangular piece of land that jutted out into the water. The architecture was accentuated by rich wood the color of fine chocolate and intricately carved details that you would find in inns in the European Alps.

Behind the inn were several quaint docks. One could board small, classic wooden launches and visit the tiny island in the center of the lake or just cruise the still, deep waters as local fisherman caught succulent trout for a fine meal.

The area is often referred to as the Switzerland of Colombia. The verdant green of the trees lining the shore reflect off the lake waters and create a picture with the quality of a fine oil painting. Since La Cocha is surrounded by mountains, if you climb up the inclines from the lake the vistas below are striking. It was this breathtaking quality that brought me to the lake that day. I wanted to take photographs that I could use for some of my stories. I also knew they would be perfect for the Colombian calendar I wanted to develop.

I set out in the Fiat with my camera bag and two young daughters, who had begged to accompany me. The drive up from Pasto was pleasant. Although unusual for the lake area, it was one of those perfect Colombian days, billows of white and black clouds racing across large patches of cobalt sky. I hoped it wouldn't close in and the light would hold. The temperature was crisp. We wound our way up to the lake, encountering little traffic.

Once there I began looking for the perfect spot to snap some panoramic pictures. First, I circled the lake road, but could not get high enough to gain the perspective and angle I wanted. By then the sky had closed and it began raining. The light was still fairly good, though, and I knew the rain would be intermittent so I pressed on.

I found a dirt road, which had turned slick and muddy with the sudden rain. Nonetheless, I started up its incline. Although the front wheel drive of the Fiat afforded excellent traction under most conditions, the road became increasingly treacherous as we climbed. Finally, right before a sharp curve, I decided it was becoming too dangerous to continue the ascent. There were no side roads so I carefully made a three point turn and headed back down.

My oldest daughter, Natalie, was in the passenger seat and my youngest, Veronica, in the back. I turned to Natalie and told her we would have an early lunch and try to figure out what to do next to get the pictures. I thought in the worst case we could come back another day.

I glanced in the rear view mirror and could see a vehicle that appeared to be fast approaching us, but with the winding road it was just an occasional glimpse. We continued down the main lake road and finally pulled into the small parking lot of the inn. That's when things started to get very crazy very fast.

No sooner had I turned off the engine when our vehicle was surrounded by three open olive green jeeps full of men in army fatigues carrying automatic weapons. All of them were aimed at us. It was so sudden

I froze and simply stared, trying to comprehend what was happening.

It started raining harder, but the armed men ignored the downpour. Water ran in rivulets off their plastic ponchos. Expressionless they looked at us, their guns pointed at the car. My nerves began to unravel. My mind raced. Why had I brought the girls? I didn't know if they were Colombian soldiers or guerrillas since they all wore the same drab olive green uniforms.

Before I could move, one of the men leaped out of the jeep parked in front of our car. He yanked open the passenger door and ordered Natalie to get in the back. Eyes wide, her mouth slightly open, she looked at me. I nodded at her, tried to muster a confident smile, and she did as she was told.

The soldier or guerrilla—I didn't know which—then climbed in and with the stock of his weapon on his lap, rested the cold metal barrel against my temple. Without thinking I pushed it away. He glared at me. I glanced back at the girls. They were frozen, just staring at me.

My captor grunted and backed the barrel of the gun off a few inches. "Drive," he commanded in Spanish.

"Where?" I asked.

As he signaled for his men to move the jeep blocking the car, he told me to follow the road I had just driven. With trembling legs I depressed the clutch, shifted into first, popped the pedal and we were off to a shaky jack rabbit start. Again my captor glared at me. I kept glancing in the rear view mirror. The girls had remained completely silent as they watched the scene play out. No doubt they were scared, but they seemed calm under the circumstances. There was no crying and no hysterics.

I am not sure I felt the same way. My mind was in overdrive with a thousand questions and concerns. Were we being kidnapped? It appeared so. How could they have known I would be at La Cocha that day? Had I been followed or was it just a chance encounter? Did they know I was a gringo? Probably. My accent was a dead giveaway. It seemed surreal. I kept asking myself how this could be happening.

My heart continued to threaten to burst out of my chest as it hammered away, but with little choice I drove on, winding up through the gears of the Fiat's five speed transmission. The armed man didn't talk, but I could feel his eyes on me. I started to slow down. I guess subconsciously I was stalling for time. I wondered if anyone from the inn had seen what happened. I doubted it. My captor gestured for me to speed up. As I did, my heart continued to sink the farther we went.

We finally reached the spot where I had turned around. The little car spun on the muddy surface fighting for traction. The three jeeps behind us hung close. I could clearly see the men in the mirror with their rifles pointing skyward or in our direction. There was no way I could lose them. Not to mention the stoic soldier with his gun still pointed at my head.

As I rounded the curve, I received my second big

shock of the day. On both sides of the road were military vehicles and more armed men. They were everywhere— fifty or more was my guess. It was a classic ambush. One we had avoided earlier because we turned around before the sharp sweep in the road.

My captor told me to pull up to a jeep where four men were standing. Once stopped, he motioned for me to get out of the car. As I climbed out slowly I told the girls not to worry and to sit tight. They simply looked at me with their wide, innocent eyes, but remained silent.

The soldier had circled around behind me and poked his rifle sharply into my back. Slightly off balance I was propelled forward toward the men. All wore soft cloth olive colored hats, dampened by the rain, but one had a gold insignia on his. With that and his confident presence, I knew immediately who was in charge.

He eyed me suspiciously for several long moments. I became aware that I had to go to the bathroom. I didn't know if this was nerves or a genuine need. Uncomfortable, I shifted slightly on my feet, and tried to maintain a neutral demeanor. I remained silent and returned his stare, trying to appear calm, although I was sure my eyes reflected real fear.

Finally he said, "Norte Americano?"

Unsure of my voice, I just nodded.

More silence followed. I could hear the ticking sound as the engine of my car cooled. I risked a glance behind me to make sure the girls were still in the car. As I turned back to face him, he asked me for my identification. I explained that my passport was in my bag in the back of the car.

He motioned for one of his men to retrieve it. His unblinking eyes never left mine as he held out his hand and received the bag. When he unsnapped the blue canvas bag I could tell he was surprised when he saw my 35 millimeter camera, boxes of film, various lenses, and other photography paraphernalia.

He looked sharply at me, but didn't speak. My blue-jacketed American passport was clearly visible tucked in the side of the main compartment of the bag, but he didn't look at it right away. Instead he hefted my Yashica, turning it over in his hands and examining it closely. Then he casually returned it to its resting place, pulled out my passport, and handed the bag to one of his men.

He opened it and did several checks between the photo and my face and then began to flip through the pages filled with visa stamps. I should note that at the time I was living in Colombia with a resident visa. On the visa was written that my occupation was escritor (writer).

He studied the visa intently then referred again to the page with my photo and name. He did this several times, glancing at me as I stood there and shifted uncomfortably from one leg to the other. I was still not sure if they were the good guys or the bad guys. My mind worked. If they were good guys, what was this all about? I had done nothing wrong.

He continued to look at the passport and I became aware that he kept softly repeating my name, as if fascinated by the sound of it. I continued to squirm a bit, probably as much from nerves as my urge to relieve myself. I was about to press my luck and demand that we be allowed to leave.

What happened next caused my jaw to drop and eyes to grow wide. Never in my wildest dreams could I have imagined it. The unexpected scene seemed to unfold before me in slow motion, but I know it all transpired in a matter of a few seconds.

I watched as the officer reached up and grasped the bill of his cap with his right hand, whipped it off his head, and took a hard swipe at the man who had been my captor, striking him with the hat. He repeatedly kept swinging his hat and hitting the man on the head and shoulders and muttering loudly, "stupido" as I looked on in amazement. To his credit, the man being assaulted barely cringed.

Finally, the officer stopped and placed his cap back on his head, which he kept shaking in disbelief. He looked at the soldier again and said in Spanish, "Stupid, this man is a famous North American writer."

That was news to me, but I was in no position to either correct him or argue. He turned to me and apologized in broken English, handing me both my camera bag and passport. I stood there unsure of what to say or do. Seeing my hesitation the officer stepped forward and grasped my arm, turning me around as he began to talk to me.

"I have heard your name. I know you are a famous writer, living in Pasto, I believe. My colonel has spoken of you."

This was a bit of an exaggeration, but things began to click into place for me. I indeed did know the colonel who ran the local military unit in Nariño. We had met at a cocktail party in my neighborhood.

I took a deep breath and as my heart rate slowed, I asked, "What was this all about, anyway? I didn't know if you were guerrillas or Colombian military forces. I thought we were being kidnapped."

He looked a little sheepish. "I trust if you talk to the colonel you will say you were treated with respect?'

"Of course. I have no complaints."

"We are here because a bank was robbed in Putumayo."

"I don't understand. Surely you didn't think I robbed it?"

"Well, there is only one road out of that area and this is it. When we saw you approach our ambush, then suddenly turn around, we naturally thought you might have seen us and were fleeing."

"And you assumed I was the thief."

"You can understand how that would be a natural assumption. But when I sent my men after you and they stopped a car with an American and two little girls they should have realized you were not the person. That is why I was angry with my man. He should have known that." He hesitated thoughtfully, shook his head, and said, "Or perhaps not."

He shrugged apologetically and that essentially ended our conversation. He seemed like a decent young soldier. I offered my hand and we shook. I told him I hoped they got their man. I gave him my card and said to call me and perhaps we could share a few drinks when he was off duty.

As it turned out we did just that several times over the following year. It was the beginning of my education and lesson number one: you couldn't have too many friends when you were the lone American in a remote part of a foreign land.

I remember him patting my shoulder as he turned back towards his men. The gesture touched me. I opened the car door and smiled at the girls. Suddenly, as if a switch had been turned on, they were full of questions, both talking at once. I explained what happened and we all laughed.

Natalie said, "Wait until we tell Mom." Shaking my head I wondered aloud if that was a good idea, but realized our adventure was probably destined to become family gossip. In my haste to start the car, I flooded it and it turned over several times before the engine came to life. I waved at my new friend and he gave me a casual salute. Once I was back down the road I stopped, pulled out my journal and recorded the details while they were fresh in my mind.

Reflecting on the incident, it was such an unexpected event, downright comical and yet scary at the same time. That day my legs would shake uncontrollably at random times. I couldn't stop thinking, what if they had been guerrillas? I remember looking at the girls and shivering, not from the chill, but from pure fear. It wasn't something I wanted to think too much about, but I was grateful that the girls hadn't seemed to grasp the potential seriousness of the situation.

It was a sobering reminder that, while I could move about with ease and write the stories I wanted, I needed to exercise some judgment and caution. As it turned out, though, it wasn't a lesson I always remembered. Later there would be times when I felt silly and naïve and wonder about the actions I sometimes took. I would also wonder if I was just looking for problems and trouble or they seemed to sometimes find me without any help.

That day, though, I shrugged it off and drove slowly home, stopping at a small roadside restaurant, instead of the inn, where we ate chicken roasted over an open fire and small potatoes crusted with salt, called papa saladas. The girls chattered excitedly the whole way home. One of the things that Natalie said was, "Dad, the soldier holding the gun on you had dirty fingernails." She still remembers that detail.

After I pulled into the driveway they leaped out of the car and raced into the house. "Mom, Mom, you are not going to believe what happened to us..." It wouldn't be the last time my understanding wife would hear those words.

2

LITTLE PEOPLE LIVING ON MEDELLIN'S STREETS

Early Spring, 1985

On an unusually warm afternoon, as was my custom when possible, I was sitting in Pasto's central plaza eating a delicious cherry flavored snow cone doused with condensed milk when a man in a black cassock sat down next to me. His face was flushed and he kept mopping his brow with a large handkerchief. After we exchanged a few pleasantries, it became clear to him that Spanish was not my native language. I was relieved to discover that he spoke English and he switched easily into my language.

He was a Catholic priest from the Salesian Order. I bought him a snow cone from the vendor in the park and we continued to chat for some time. Our conversation finally centered on his mission to save impoverished children. The story of his work was fascinating and heart wrenching. Mesmerized, I felt completely drawn to write about it.

I didn't realize it at that moment, but to write the story I would spend a few nights sleeping in the streets and sewers with street kids to try and capture their experiences and environment. It was both disturbing and interesting. They live a life that is unimaginable unless you actually try to walk in their shoes, if only for a brief period. Many live the life of a modern day "Oliver Twist."

Three days later I flew from Nariño to Medellin on assignment to research and write a story about street kids for the largest Catholic newspaper in the United States.

Medellin, with a population of about 3 million, is one of the main industrial and commerce centers in Colombia, especially for textiles. A city of universities, world class medical research and facilities, and a global exporter of flowers, it was also the home of many of the country's most powerful drug lords, including the notorious Pablo Escobar. I can only compare this prevalence of mafia families to their Italian counterparts concentrated in Sicily.

After landing I could see why everyone had told me that it was a city of eternal spring. The weather was perfect, like a spring day in New York. The temperature then dipped to crisp at night. I took a taxi to a facility run by Salesian priests. It was established to help get the large number of parentless kids off the streets.

The following is adapted from a story I filed at the time, capturing this episode. Not much has changed. Except for the cast of characters the story is the same.

Colombian Street Kids[2]

Gamines, or waifs, roam in groups; like miniature vagabonds they live in the streets. By age 10 they have probably experienced sex, drugs, violence, the thrill of stealing, capture, and escape. The odds are also good that they have killed or assaulted someone. Fiercely independent, the gamines of Colombia share many traits of "Oliver." They may even be working for a Latin version of "Fagin."

There are thousands on Colombian streets, where, according to Greg Caput (an American who worked there at the time this story was published), "…it is dangerous even for adults. Imagine being a kid and having to call them home."

Yet, there is a light that shines brightly. Under the guidance of Salesian missionaries and volunteers, many kids are being reached and are transforming their lives. The ambitious program began in 1980 and now operates in most the country's

---

2 Adapted from "Salesians Transform Lives of Colombian Waifs," Our Sundayz Visitor, October 20, 1985, by Michael F. Kastre

major cities. In Medellin, Colombia's second largest city, the Salesians have two facilities dedicated to this purpose. The "Patio" is located downtown and serves as the door in from the cold for street kids. From there they can go on to a model boys' town called Cuidad Don Bosco.

Caput is one of six Salesian Volunteers from the US. A tall lanky man, he has an easy manner with the gamines. For over two years he has worked at the Patio. Inside the brick entrance is a scruffy tan and red tile floor surrounded by white and gray walls. Access to the courtyard beyond is through a battered wooden door. The windows are barred with ornate wrought iron. At first glance it seems like a grim beginning for a new life, but it holds hope and love for those who enter.

"Getting the kids to come in from the streets is the toughest problem," Caput said. He added, "They can come here to wash, eat lunch, and play a game of soccer, but surprisingly many prefer to remain in the streets and beg or steal food."

Their lives have endowed them with a savvy beyond their years. Nine-year old Bolivar explained his outlook by saying, "Sometimes I think I will return to the streets. I miss being there." He grinned, "If you learn responsibility you can't be free because after that you feel funny, you know, guilty when you don't do something you know is right."

"We try to help kids from ages five to fifteen," Caput said. "Every four months twenty-five boys can opt to go on and live at Don Bosco where they can study and learn a trade. First, though, they must come regularly to the Patio. It's days only, no boys live here. It's here that they learn to give and receive and to make a commitment. Later they will learn to be productive and help themselves. That's really what we want to give them."

The morning I arrived, there were about thirty boys milling around the Patio, washing clothes and eating lunch. Caput was handing out vitamins and trying to organize a soccer game.

Later in the day I was taken to Cuidad Don Bosco. As we left downtown, the streets became narrow, twisting and winding up out of the valley. They finally gave way to a steep, almost impassible dirt road. The boys' town was an attractive brick complex with red tile roofs and sat atop a hill overlooking the city.

It was named for St. John Bosco, the 19th century priest who founded the Salesian Order. His life's work was dedicated to helping homeless youth, not merely by providing bread, but through education, thereby giving them the means to help themselves. The Salesians were carrying on that tradition.

The difference between the battered Patio, with its unkempt, boisterous kids, and the Cuidad was striking. The clean, neatly dressed boys who surrounded me presented an entirely different picture. With pride they showed me the dormitories, chapel, classrooms, and small store. Don Bosco had wood and metal shops where the boys made their furniture and learned various skills. A tailor shop produced much of the clothing.

In the valley below, dusk was settling over the city. I was told it was time to go into the streets with Father Echandia, Caput, and another Salesian volunteer, Andy Powell. We started at Bolivar Park for what would be a three-hour walk. Eventually we ended up close to the Patio.

Earlier in the daylight the streets of the poor neighborhood had looked normal enough, bustling traffic, people hurrying to work, the blare of horns, and street vendors hawking their wares. By night, however, another world emerges, a world few people ever see, the tragic shadow world of the gamines. Kids as young as four or five share the street corners with adult prostitutes, winos, and drug addicts. The smell of urine and poverty permeates the air around the alleys and side streets.

Groups of kids greeted the Salesians with hugs and handshakes. In dark sidewalks and alleys kids huddled together for the long night. Some were wrapped in newspapers and stretched out in doorways, scrawny bodies stacked on top of one another for protection against the cold and sexual assaults. Grimy dirt-caked feet poked out from tattered dresses and trousers. Smells once associated with such places as New York's Bowery permeated the air. Over half of the kids seemed high on drugs, their large brown eyes unfocused, their speech slurred. Half-filled pint bottles were stuffed up their sleeves.

"It's a mixture of shoe glue and acetone and is cheap and easy to obtain," Caput told me. He added, "The acetone releases the toxic fumes at an accelerated rate. Sniffed over a long enough period of time it kills."

Four boys emerged from a storm drain by a bus stop. They clustered around Caput and Father Echandia. All had the familiar glue bottle. The adults kept trying to coax them into giving up the deadly mixture for a least the night. The kids were friendly in a drunken way, but finally retreated down the drains, the oldest sliding the cement cover into place.

Father Echandia estimated that there were over 1,500 gamines in the city. "They are most visible in el central (downtown), but many more are concealed in the sprawling barrios that flank the city," he said.

When asked why the program seemed to focus almost exclusively on boys, he replied, "There is a program for girls, which is run by the Salesian Sisters. In numbers, girls account for only about twenty percent of the gamines, but they are tougher than the boys. They have to be to survive. The biggest problem is prostitution," the boyish blond priest added.

He continued, "Once a girl of six or seven is on the streets and into glue-sniffing or other drugs, it's almost impossible to break the cycle. By eight or nine they have had sex; by ten or eleven they are selling

their bodies on a regular basis. When they
have reached twelve or thirteen they have
a baby and are perhaps pregnant again."

Powell tried to talk a little boy of about
eight into coming the next day to the Patio
for some talk and lunch. In his drunken
stupor the boy didn't seem to understand.
After he had staggered away, Powell asked
me, "How would you like to be seven years
old and wake up every day of your life with
a hangover?"

With no answer, I could only stare at
him.

At ten-thirty that night we caught the
bus back to Cuidad Don Bosco and trudged up
the steep driveway. I asked why we didn't
stay later or even spend the night on the
streets and keep trying to convince the
kids to come into the Patio. I was told
that the experience of the Salesians was
that by that time most of the kids were too
high to reason with.

I was unsatisfied because I really had
not talked to the gamines as much as I
wanted. Once inside the dormitory-like
residence for the priests and volunteers,
I sat in the dark in my Spartan room for
about 30 minutes and then slipped quietly
out. I drifted back down the hill and

caught a taxi to downtown. It was a routine I would repeat for several nights. All alone without the company and savvy of the priest and volunteers I was nervous, but determined to find out more. Adrenaline coursed through my body and I forced myself to slow down my breathing to calm myself.

I approached the area where the kids had disappeared into the city's sewer system. With my heart pounding I slid back an access cover and descended into darkness, fighting to control my claustrophobic tendencies. I stood very still and could hear the murmur of alarmed voices. I flipped open my lighter and the immediate surroundings were illuminated in weak flickering light. In as calm a voice as I could muster, I assured the unseen little people that I only wanted to talk.

Finally, a boy of about eleven or twelve merged into the light and said he recognized me from earlier. He was slender with unruly black hair. His cheeks were unnaturally flushed and his dark eyes hard. His manner alternated between aggressive and defensive. I met his gaze and asked if he would be willing to talk to me. At first he just stared at me. After some thought, he consented if I would give him some pesos.

Then he stepped quickly forward and grasped the front of my shirt. Although completely off guard, I didn't resist when he drew me along for several yards. With my heart beating wildly I stumbled along in the dark, flicking my lighter on and off several times because it became too hot to hold.

He slid down the sloping walls and I did the same. As we partially reclined in the dark, I could sense others—how many I didn't know—the rustle of clothes, whispers. Gradually the soft sounds subsided as they seemed to sense that the danger was past and settled in for the night.

My "host," as it were, seemed somewhat high, but coherent and wide awake. "Tell me about yourself," I urged.

In a gentle, slightly slurred voice he told me his story about being abandoned by his parents when he was nine. His specialty was picking pockets. Although in the soft light he did show me a sinister looking knife that he flipped open with casual efficiency. He said he used it occasionally for armed robberies of small stores and assaults on unsuspecting pedestrians.

At some point he dozed off. Quietly, I

left the tunnel and returned to the street. That morning before dawn broke over the city, I returned to Cuidad Don Bosco stiff, dirty, and totally depressed. I was able to slip in to the complex undetected.

I would meet my young contact and talk to him several more nights, during which time he introduced me to a boy a couple of years older who claimed to have murdered several victims for money. According to this little hit man, an unscrupulous guy who operated several taxis was the conduit through which these contract murders were set up.

When I first asked the young criminal about the victims he simply shrugged. The casual manner in which this was done was chilling. When pressed he told me that one was a business rival who had cheated his contact out of a large sum of money. Another was a minor political player who for whatever reason was murdered. No matter how hard I pushed, that was all he was willing to divulge.

He felt no remorse. "Why should he?" he asked. After all, he explained, a certain segment of the moneyed main stream population often hunted him and his fellow gamines for sport. When asked, he said that on a regular basis cabs and trucks would cruise through the barrio at night. Automatic windows would be lowered and shots would ring out.

"They shoot us like rats," he said.

I asked why?

He shrugged and replied, "Who knows? The thrill? To rid the city of us? I don't know, but it happens."

I wasn't sure I believed him at that moment. Later, though, I asked the Salesians about this and they confirmed that it did indeed happen. Their answer as to why was no more satisfying than that of the young waif. It was more of a verbal shrug that said, "who knows."

At the time, the director of Cuidad Don Bosco was Father Montalvo, a big imposing man with closely cropped curly hair. I spent several mornings talking to him. I remember that unlike the turbulent street life of the city below, those days at the boy's town were peaceful. The air was filled with the smell of freshly cut wood and the whine of power saws from the shops.

From Montalvo's eyes I could tell that his years of experience with street kids had not made his mission any easier. They were eyes that had seen too much of this unseemly and hidden side of life.

He told me, "The problem is complicated, but not difficult to understand. It's socio-economic. People from the country come to the cities in search of a better life. Usually they are large families, seven to fifteen people. There are few if any jobs for them that pay decent money, so they end up crowded into a shack in a shanty town with intolerable conditions. To escape, the kids turn to the streets, drugs, and crime. That's one way. Since it's one less mouth to feed, the parents may actually be relieved if a kid runs away…"

He continued, "The other story is a man who might have three or four kids with the same woman. With little money and living a miserable life, he turns to alcohol. Eventually he deserts them only to find another woman and repeat the cycle. He may do this many times with different women."

He shook his head, "It's a time when the [Catholic] Church needs to exert more influence on people in teaching responsibility, love and respect. People here are faced with an economic crisis and a crisis in the basic family unit. The result can be seen with the gamines. These are not just kids, they are abandoned kids…"

The irony is that Colombia is a Catholic country. Accordingly, it's no secret that the Church opposes birth control and abortion. It's also a failure in the basic education system in a country where the Church profoundly impacts the operation of public schools. (Religious control of the schools continues despite numerous constitutional changes intended to establish a separation of government and church. This is a result of the strong influence exerted by the powerful Catholic Church. Clerics often wield their power through historical and interpersonal relationships. This unofficial authority permeates the entire public school system.)

To many Americans, such a situation may seem incomprehensible. But in this regard, Colombians see us as hypocrites. Ask a Colombian about it and odds are they will become defensive. Then they will rightfully point to exploding rates of teenage pregnancy in the US. They will also point to our failing education system. They are mystified, and often angry, questioning how we can judge them when we ourselves suffer many of the same problems.

Our social safety net may be wider so that the problems don't manifest themselves on the same level as those posed by Colombian gamines; but we still have our share of runaways who live a life of prostitution, crime, and drugs.

So, while most Colombians admire the US, and indeed, many seek to immigrate for more opportunities, they find a certain arrogance and hypocrisy in our perspective and how we judge others. This is moderated by their fascination with America in a clear conflict of emotions.

One thing they are quick to point out, and I personally observed it. That is, for the most part Colombia is a country whose very fabric is held together by the prominent role that family plays. In reality, the overwhelming majority of Colombians are part of strong families—both rich and poor.

Cuidad don Bosco still exists and is carrying on its good works of providing a safe haven for street boys. Now, as then, it survives by receiving support from individuals and national and international organizations. But it is the Salesian priests and volunteers who continue to provide the resolve, energy, and spiritual strength that enables the program to provide hope to a segment of the population with few champions.

I left Medellin feeling an odd mixture of sadness tinged with a touch of optimism. My restless unease was pushed to the back of my mind as I arrived at the airport to find total chaos with the start of a national transportation strike. With a little luck, though, I finally managed to board a plane late in the day.

3

TORCHING THE PALACE OF JUSTICE

November 6, 1985

How I ended up in the wrong place at the wrong time to witness one of the most shockingly violent episodes in Colombian history was a simple matter of random banking.

Unlike today, in 1980s Colombia there were no ATMs to disperse money. Instead you either had to cash a check, which no one would accept since mine wasn't just out of town, but out of the country, or have cash. I didn't have any bank accounts in the country since the money I made writing was paid to me by check in the US. Nonetheless, I paid all my expenses in pesos, including things like rent and food.

At first I used a simple system. Every few months I would fly to the US and deposit the checks that were waiting for me. Then I would get a few thousand dollars in cash and return home to Colombia.

As I mention earlier in the book, before moving to Colombia I had built a large wooden wine cabinet on casters. In the base I had bolted a strong box and that became the safe where I stored a few months' worth of dollars. When I needed money I had to go to the Bank of the Republic—which was the only official place at that time—and change dollars into pesos. I tried to change only what I needed in the short term because the inflation rate in Colombia was high and I wanted to take advantage of the escalating dollar. Indeed, during my time in Colombia the dollar more than doubled versus the peso.

That was my banking system. With time, though, frequent trips to the US became increasingly difficult because of time and money. I started having my checks for stories from publishers sent to my dad. He would then stamp them "for deposit only" and put them into my account. That, however, didn't really solve the problem of how to actually get my hands on the money when I needed it without traveling to the States.

My problem was solved one day when I met a British gentleman named Basil in a bar in Bogota. We chatted and it turned out that Basil was the manager of the Banco Anglo Colombiano in Bogota. I never fully understood the relationship, but apparently they were an affiliate with a sister banking company in London, which is how an English chap ended up being the manager of a bank in Colombia.

No matter. I learned that Basil had an account in the

US. When I explained my dilemma, he was more than willing to take my personal checks and give me pesos in return. He would then send the checks to his account in the US. He got dollars and I got pesos. Problem solved.

After my agreement with Basil I would periodically drive or fly from Pasto to Bogota to get money for my living and operating expenses. It sure beat a round trip to the US just to cash a check or withdraw cash.

November 6 was one such occasion with the day starting innocently enough. It was midmorning when I walked the 25 blocks from where we were staying at my in-laws' home in the northern section of Bogota, called Polo Club, to downtown. It was about a 45 minute walk to Basil's building, which was located a couple of blocks northeast of the Plaza de Bolivar.

Bounded by Carrera 7 on the eastern side, Calle 10 on the south, Carrera 8 on the west, and Calle 11 on the north side, the Plaza is a huge open area that is the seat of Colombia's political, judicial, and religious activities.

Although not quite laid out on the points of the compass, the general north side of the Plaza is dominated by the Palacio de Justicia (Colombia's Supreme Court); the National Cathedral, consisting of several connected chapels—Cathedral Primada, Capilla del Sagrario, and Palacio Arzobispal—is situated on the eastern edge; the Capitolio Nacional (Capitol building), which houses the National Congress fronts the southern portion; and the Palacio Lievano on the west, which is the city's

Alcaldia (mayor's office). Casa Nariño, the Colombian equivalent of the White House, lays a couple of blocks south of the Plaza.

A few minutes after arriving at Basil's outer office, I heard gunfire and mass confusion to the south, in the direction of the Plaza. At that point, I no idea what was going on, but I slung my ever present camera bag over my shoulder and hurried back out of the building. I headed down Carrera 8 toward the main Plaza.

I could hear shots and men shouting. About halfway down the northwest side of the Justice Palace, looking southeast, I could see men in army uniforms. The shots grew increasingly louder and I ducked into an alcove on the side of the building.

Because of my position I couldn't see the front of the court building, where all of the gun fire seemed to be coming from. Nonetheless, I pulled out my camera and started shooting film. Periodically I would poke my head out and shoot to my left then alternate and shoot to my right.

A large angry crowd had started to gather on Carrera 8 at Calle 12 by the northwest corner of the court building. Looking down the street they faced a growing group of what would turn out to be armed soldiers and police. Periodically, the crowd would surge down the street throwing bottles and rocks in the direction of the government troops at the southwest corner of the building. The crowd would charge forward, tossing their projectiles, and then retreat as the soldiers in turn surged towards them. This became a pattern.

I didn't understand why the crowd was unruly and angry. It made no sense to me why they were attacking the government troops. Moreover, trapped in my no man's land between the two factions, I still had no idea what was happening in the Plaza. I just kept sticking my head out and shooting left and right.

I lost all sense of time. I believe it was early afternoon when it appeared as though the military was

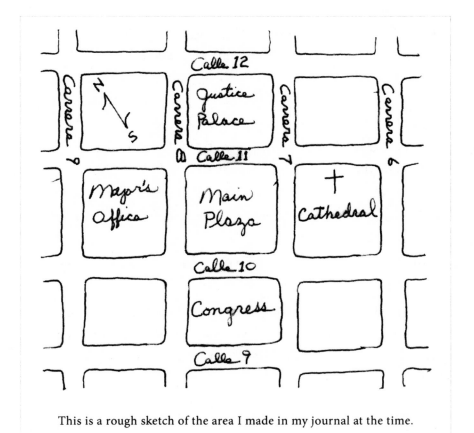

This is a rough sketch of the area I made in my journal at the time.

growing increasingly tired of the crowd and moved to do something decisive. Before that they had maintained about a block's separation (the length of the court building) from the crowd—with me in the middle.

I could sense it as they advanced further down the side of the building, getting closer to my position as they moved to drive the crowd back. When the group of armed men came abreast of me, I must have looked like a deer caught in headlights. Some of the soldiers kept advancing, but the officer who appeared to be in charge stopped in front of me with a handful of men. At first his features registered surprise. This quickly changed as he glared angrily at me and pointed a pistol at my midsection. I immediately raised my hands, my camera gripped tightly in one.

Mortality is tough to process for most people. Throughout my life, it certainly has been for me. During that moment, though, I remember doing my best to put mine into perspective. I honestly don't know what emotions I experienced, though I suspect it was an equal parts mixture of fear, panic, and excitement, all fueled by adrenaline. One thing for sure was that for one of the rare times in my life I was certain I was going to die—shot in the excitement of some crazy event unfolding around me that I didn't even understand at that moment.

He pushed the gun roughly into my gut and asked who I was. I stuttered and tried to explain. Lowering his pistol and holding it in one hand, he reached up and grabbed my camera. As he did I managed to trip the back panel, exposing the 35mm film. I remember this because I was afraid he would smash the camera to the pavement. My thinking was that by opening the camera body he might only strip the film out, which he did. All the while he berated me and asked who I was.

This confusion and animated dialog went on for a few minutes. Finally, he thrust the camera into my hands and said something to his men. I was grasped by both arms and led down Carrera 8 to Calle 11 where we turned right. I recall we skirted the chaos less than a block over and I found myself by the Inglesia Santa Clara, a jewel box of a church, which had been converted to a museum to showcase its ornate interior. This placed us at the southwest corner of the capitol building, on the opposite end of the Plaza, but out of the line of fire.

Events became a blur as I repeated my story to various officials as soldiers came and went, reporting in on what was happening. From their words I gathered that there was an attack by guerrillas on the Supreme Court. I had visions of being escorted to some dark cell in a nearby prison while things were sorted out.

Unexpectedly, I was approached by an older officer with a calm demeanor and tired eyes. Finally, I thought, some sanity and decided at last that they had realized I was who I said I was and that I had merely stumbled into the middle of the assault. My hope was rewarded as he told me I was free to go. He told me that I should leave the area immediately and sternly cautioned me that I was not to return. It was after dark as I was escorted down Calle 9 where it intersected with Carrera 10, which is a large boulevard one block over and two blocks down from the Plaza.

The streets were quickly becoming deserted as people scurried away from the area. I learned a short time later that a curfew was in effect. Anyone caught on the street was subject to arrest. I started walking quickly and eventually found myself close to the Hotel Tequendama in front of a bar, which I promptly entered. I had a few drinks, avoiding conversation with the bartender and customers, all of whom were talking excitedly about the day's events.

I wanted to contact my wife, but there were precious few payphones. It occurred to me she was probably more than a little worried. I was late and she knew that I had left that morning bound for a location very close to the Plaza. I left the bar. By that time the streets were deserted—no people, cars, buses, or taxis. I started walking again and sometime around 10 pm that night I arrived at the home of my in-laws.

My wife was relieved to say the least and I recounted what I had experienced. My fear had abated and I was upset at the loss of what I knew were a unique set of photos. I started planning another foray downtown early the next morning and to her credit, my wife agreed to accompany me.

By 7 am we were headed downtown. We got as close

as possible by cab and started walking. It didn't take long before we were engulfed by the angry crowd—by this time numbering in the thousands—I had seen the day before. It was like being in an ocean. If the tide surged one way or the other, we were powerless to move and were helplessly swept along. After a couple of times of being propelled forward and then backwards, we were both starting to panic.

We fought our way to the edge of the unruly mass. We realized it was probably going to be impossible to get close so we started looking for a tall building as a vantage point to take photos. We talked our way into the Avianca airlines building and took some pictures, but it was too far from the action.

By early afternoon on the following day, after 27 hours, the siege was over. Almost half the members of the Supreme Court had been slaughtered, as were many others—an estimated 110 in total. And the building that housed the Supreme Court had been set ablaze, gutted, and all records destroyed, including drug czar extradition case files.

What Happened & Why

Amid a swirling storm of charges, countercharges, rumors, and conspiracy theories, I started to piece together and sort out what had actually happened. The basic facts of "what" happened, though, are fairly straightforward as compared to the "why" it happened.

Supposedly, the siege took place when the building

was relatively unprotected because the pending attack was allegedly known in advance by authorities. So, it was set up as an enticing trap for the rebels. (This, of course, begs the obvious questions: If the government knew, why didn't they make sure the judges were not in the building? Or, why didn't they place troops inside the building?)

No matter if this is true or false, what is known is that M-19 rebels arrived at the plaza in a stolen truck. The heavily armed men burst into Palace, killing the building's administrator and the few security guards and taking 300 people hostage. These included 24 justices and 20 judges. Among these was Chief Justice Alfonso Reyes.

Confusion reigned for several hours after as the military poured into the area. A recording delivered to a local radio station said the M-19 had taken over the building "in the name of peace and social justice." (I am always fascinated when a group commits violence in the name of peace and social justice.) Eventually, troops fought their way into the building, rescuing approximately 200 hostages from the first three floors of the Palace. The surviving rebels retreated to the upper two floors, taking the remaining hostages.

It was later reported that Chief Justice Reyes was allowed to communicate with officials on the outside and unsuccessfully sought a negotiated rescue with then Colombian President Belasario Betancur. Instead, Betancur turned the whole affair over to the military to handle. In the meantime, he went on national TV the night of November 7th and took responsibility for the "terrible nightmare." Yet, when it was unfolding the Colombian military continued to shoot, despite the urgent pleas of the magistrates being held in the building.

The military patrols the area near the Justice Palace after the attack.

I talked to many officials and Colombians during that time and in the ensuing years. In my mind, though, questions remained: Did the military or the rebels— or both—kill Reyes and 10 other justices? Or, was it simply the result of the deadly crossfire between troops and rebels? This and other issues are still being debated and investigated today.

What is known is that all 35 rebels were killed,

including guerrilla leader Andres Almarales and a handful of senior commanders. In addition, 46 soldiers died along with dozens of civilians.

It's also a fact that to gain access to the Palace, the army drove a heavily armored vehicle with a turret— much like a tank with tires—into the Plaza and blasted down the massive main doors. Troops poured in and a fierce fire fight followed. Finally, with the building a smoldering mess, it was over.

The operation was under the command of General Arias, who in turn assigned Colonel Alfonso Plazas to personally oversee the operation. The colonel's actions, though, created a controversy which continues to this day. In fact, ongoing investigations into the tragedy concluded that some civilians who left the Palace under Plazas' command were never seen again. As a result, Plazas, now retired, was sentenced in 2010 to 30 years in prison after being found guilty in connection with making people disappear after the assault on the Palace 25 years before.

Prior to Plazas' legal troubles, another soldier and military intelligence officer named Ivan Ramirez— also known as the godfather of Colombian army intelligence—was arrested and indicted with what the prosecutor called "forced disappearance." The charges were based on eye witness accounts, including some from soldiers of his unit, who said that Ramirez directed the torture and killing of some captives at the Justice Palace after which the bodies were made to disappear. Ramirez was, however, acquitted in 2011. The exoneration came despite strong evidence against him, including not only the eye witness accounts, but declassified US embassy cables linking Ramirez to the disappearances as well.

Even though the Supreme Court's Truth Commission is still investigating, as of the writing of this book, there seem to be more questions than answers. Not surprisingly there are many theories still circulating and impacting current Colombian politics. And events such as the sentencing of Plazas only reinforce people's mistrust of official accounts as they struggle to understand the often hidden and surprising relationships among justice officials, politicians, drug czars, guerrillas, and the military.

I have long tried to understand why, or what drove the events of that day. For example, when I was trapped between the military and the people, why was the crowd attacking the government forces with everything they could hurl at them? Was it because they were sympathetic with the rebels? Or, was it because of the rumors of military abuse and cover-up, which recently reinforced by the conviction of Colonel Plazas, who led the charge that day? Or, was it a combination of factors?

I don't know and I'm not sure I believe those who say they do. What I do know is that much of the violence in 1980s Colombia was driven by the collaboration between Marxist rebels and drug czars and aided by a faction of unscrupulous politicians and judges.

This link, though, is not without dispute. The Special Commission of Inquiry into the Palace of Justice tragedy, for example, which was established by then President Betancur under intense public pressure, concluded in its 1986 report that no such relationship between the mafia and the rebels existed.

This simply wasn't true. These dangerous partnerships started before when funds for the various Colombian guerrilla groups began to dry up as the Soviet Union collapsed. It was part of a ripple effect. Up to that point, the Russians had pumped billions of dollars into Cuba, who in turn, were the primary source of financial aid and providers of weapons and ideology to Marxists revolutionaries in the Americas, including Colombia.

It should be noted, however, that even though funding was becoming scarce, other communists in the Americas still provided support to Colombian rebels. The Colombian government, for example, would later state that some of the rifles used in the assault on the Palace belonged to the Marxist Sandinista government in Nicaragua. They provided serial numbers to prove it. Colombian intelligence agents even traced the weapons to a shipment the Venezuelan government sent to the Sandinistas.

The second most obvious fact is that the day of the attack, the Supreme Court was beginning deliberations on the constitutionality of the Colombia-United States

Extradition Treaty. That seems to have set the stage. Not only did the ensuing battle with the M-19 disrupt those proceedings, but the extradition records were destroyed as well.

This was a period defined by the Medellin Cartel, whose leaders Pablo Escobar, Carlos Lehder, Gonzalo Rodriguez Gacha, and Jorge Luis Ochoa, impacted much of Colombian life related to politics and the legal system. Ledher, for instance, founded both a newspaper and a political party. And Escobar was actually elected to the Congress in 1982. When he was still relatively unknown, Escobar first attempted to break into politics through the new liberalism political movement of Luis Carlos Galan. But after Galan learned that the source of Escobar's wealth was drug trafficking, he disassociated himself from the mafia leader. Galan was later assassinated in 1989 while running for president.

Of all the billionaire mafia leaders, the undisputed drug kingpin was Escobar. At the time he was arguably the most ruthless and wealthy criminal on the planet. At the peak of his power, he had an estimated wealth of $25 billion and his Medellin drug cartel controlled 80 percent of the global cocaine market. But he was not without his Achilles' heel. Besides his lifelong fear for his family's safety was his fear of extradition to face the American justice system. He reportedly liked to say, "Better a grave in Colombia than a cell in the US." His fear was not unfounded. He had seen Ledher arrested and extradited to America where he was tried, convicted, and imprisoned.

So, bringing to an end the Extradition Treaty became like a holy grail to Escobar. To change it he tried to bring Colombia to the brink of a civil war. He, along with the Ochoas, clearly seemed to understand that the destruction, or at the very least intimidation of, the judicial system was the key. Later I would learn that Escobar and his associates paid M-19 rebels $5million to attack the high court to disrupt the extradition process (Chapter 8). In my mind this completely discredited the conclusions by President Betancur's Special Commission.

This link was consistent with Escobar's methods. He bribed the judges he could and murdered those he couldn't. He purportedly would tell them you have a choice of lead or silver—bullet or bribe. The judges' lives were not the only thing Escobar threatened to end. He also threatened their entire families and reinforced this message by sending the judges photos of their children and spouses going about their normal daily routines.

While much is known of what was going on at the time, the tragedy that occurred on November 6, 1985 in the Justice Palace remains the source of speculation and discussion among Colombians, as do ongoing investigations for the whole truth—not just the official version. Although of a different nature, it would only be one week later before another tragedy of horrific proportions would strike Colombia.

4
23,000 SOULS VANISH
November 13, 1985

A week after the tragedy at Colombia's Supreme Court I was still in Bogota chasing rumors and conspiracies when nature conspired to cause more pain to a nation already reeling from a blow to its very stability and sanity. Here is one of the stories I filed describing what happened.

Colombia Struggles to Recover from a Volcanic Disaster[3]

The 18,000 feet high Nevado del Ruiz volcano, its cone layered with snow, dominates Colombia's Central Andes mountain range. Early in the afternoon of November 13, 1985, the volcano came thunderously

---

3　Excerpted from Colombia Struggles to Recover from a Volcanic Disaster, by Michael F. Kastre, published in Our Sunday Visitor, April 20, 1986.

alive. The surrounding countryside echoed
with what sounded like muffled cannon
fire. In a fertile valley 30 miles away,
at an elevation of 1,000 feet, the 35,000
residents of Armero were blanketed with
several inches of sand and ash. The smell
of sulfur filled the air. Local radio
reports said that the volcano had erupted,
but there was no cause for alarm.

The afternoon passed. Theresa Diaz, 32,
went with her mother and two children,
aged 7 and 9, to celebrate evening Mass in
San Lorenzo. They left the church at 7:30.
Children were playing in the streets with
the mixture of sandy ash. Theresa remembers,
"The air was heavy, but everything seemed
safe and calm."

Shortly after 9 p.m. another explosion
rocked the volcano, sending a red plume
over five miles into the sky. Tons of snow
and ice, dislodged by the blast and melted
by hot lava, came rumbling down the sides
of the volcano. It followed the Lagunilla
River canyon, forming into a mile-wide
wall of hot mud, rocks, and uprooted trees.
It reached speeds of 30 miles per hour
and depths of 50 feet, hitting Armero
at about 11 p.m. With the exception of
a few houses on the edge of town, Armero

disappeared—23,000 people dead, 5,000 buildings and 2,500 vehicles buried under tons of mud and debris. The five story steeple of San Lorenzo was barely visible, with only a few inches of the cross that crowned it protruding through the mud.

Although badly damaged, the Diaz home was one of the fortunate structures on the outskirts. Theresa's mother said, "There were brilliant flashes and sparks as the wave of mud knocked over power poles. We struggled to get my invalid husband to the second floor. From the balcony I saw people being swept along the street in the mud. One man was close; I leaned out, reaching for his hand. It was slippery with mud and I couldn't hold on. I can't describe the fear and the horror. My oldest granddaughter, 11 years old, was not home at the time. She was visiting in another part of town. We still don't know if she is alive or dead."

Buildings and families were torn violently apart. Children, whose clothing was ripped from their bodies, were taken to emergency centers. With no identification papers, many became separated from what family was left—orphaned and homeless. For days, in an effort to reunite survivors, pictures flashed across TV screens, giving locations and phone numbers.

Some were saved only to be lost again. Photographer Enrique Camargo Quinones was one of the first to reach Armero. He watched in horror as people were pulled from the sticky mud. Many were hysterical; once rescued they ran off, only to be swallowed up again by the earth before they could be led to firm ground and safety.

The small Catholic city was a major economic force in the federal department of Tolima. The mud wave killed its thriving agricultural economy, destroying 50,000 acres of rich farmland, 22,000 head of cattle, and 40,000 tons of un-harvested rice and sorghum.

The only structures spared damage were a farm-supply store and house. The avalanche passed on both sides of the cluster of buildings. In front of them stands a life-size statue of the Virgin Mary.

Estimates vary, but Dr. Nelson Rengifo Valencia, secretary to Tolima's governor, said, "We believe there were 10 to 12 thousand survivors. Since recently compiled census data were destroyed in the disaster, the exact number is difficult to determine."

According to Archbishop Jose Joaquin Flores, "Armero had two parishes, San

Lorenzo and San Carmen. It was also home for two religious orders working at a school and a hospital. They were the Terciarias Capuchinas (Third Order of the Sisters of the Hooded Cloak) and the Siervas del Santisimo (Servants of the Sacred Sacrament). Three were killed."

A street block left standing after the mudslide.

Archbishop Flores is head of the Archdiocese of Ibague, Tolima's capital. He is a gentle man, soft-spoken, with salt-and-pepper hair. It has been his concern to coordinate church relief efforts. He said, "Many children were among the survivors, for them life must continue in a fashion as normal as possible. We have added two to three class periods per day in the local Catholic schools to accommodate the continuance of their education."

He paused, "The real tragedy is the children of all ages who are now alone, having possibly lost both parents and brothers and sisters. We are trying to place children with families. We are opposed to putting them into institutions, although, many are being temporarily housed by Bienestar Familiar" (Colombia's social and health agency).

Flores continued, "The loss and the task of helping was, and still is, monumental. Father Fabian Marulandia is head of our emergency services. In each town, committees were organized to help give a Christian burial to those whose bodies could be recovered. Many thousands of others are buried forever in Armero. It has been blessed and declared Campo Santo Cementario (Holy Field). Of course, we set up special Masses, especially at Christmas time. And, we are doing what we can to find housing and jobs for the survivors until the government can build popular housing. Many people are still living in tents or with relatives in other cities."

He said that the churches would be rebuilt. "Certainly not in Armero, I don't think anything will be built there again. San Lorenzo will be rebuilt somewhere else. We don't however, have plans to rebuild San Carmen." He leaned forward in his chair. "We have received help from many sources, but much still needs to be done. The Catholic Relief Fund has been a big help."

All of the houses and structures are buried beneath a barren plain in forty to fifty feet of mud. For months people continued to visit the site where the city vanished as if they hoped that some sign of the once thriving little city would miraculously reappear.

Maria Leosneida, general secretary of the Archdiocesan Pastoral Services, told me, "Father Federico Fernandez, of the Catholic Relief Fund from San Antonio, Texas, came here on January 4, 1986. The fund has given $50,000 in emergency aid. It has been divided up for farm aid and caring for the elderly and children." She added, "One severe problem is potable water, because the rivers are contaminated. Reinaldo Rozo is coordinator for a water pump program sponsored by the Catholic Church."

Three months to the day on February

13, a Mass was celebrated in Armero by Monsignor Marco Lomo Bonilla at the site where the San Lorenzo church once stood. It was a hot muggy Thursday. Thousands came to participate in the Mass and gaze at the land that was their community. Many shook their heads in disbelief. It seemed an impossible place for a tragedy. Nevado del Ruiz was far away, hidden behind the mountains, its cone covered almost perpetually in clouds.

The survivors sifted through the few ruins and debris, looking for papers, photos, or anything to remember the way it was. The desolate, broad plain, now marked only with white crosses, once had comfortable whitewashed homes with red tile roofs, streets lined by tall trees, shady parks with flowers and the squeals of children playing games.

One old man stood, stoop-shouldered, where four crosses poked out of the spongy soil. He wept for his daughter and grandchildren, his voice so choked with anguish he could not say their names.

Fifteen miles away from Armero is the town of Lerida. On its outskirts, a new pueblo is taking shape. The government has begun work on 77 houses. Hundreds more will be needed, but it is a start.

Survivor Norberto Gil, father of eight, was sitting on his small patio, working at his trade. Norberto is a shoemaker. In Armero he also worked as a caretaker and guard at San Lorenzo. Farther down the street, life has also begun anew for others. Four-day-old Carmen Julia was the first baby born in the new town. Her mother was pregnant during the disaster. She survived and gave birth to the healthy girl.

Planning and progress have been sluggish as authorities grapple with trying to organize to meet the needs of the survivors. Many refugees are unhappy with what has been done so far. They complain that programs should move faster. On several occasions, they have taken to the streets to protest their plight. This puts the Church in an awkward position because its officials are working closely with the governor's office. Yet, the archbishop is in a better position than the government to see the suffering and sympathize with those in pain and desperate need of basic services.

On February 17, Pedro Gomez, the president of the country's reconstruction efforts, appeared on national TV in an effort to quiet rumors of financial mismanagement and theft of supplies sent by the international

community. He said, "Our books are open to
all." His critics, however, point out that
three months have passed and little has
been accomplished.

Two days after Gomez's TV appearance, a
meeting was held in the department capital
of Ibague. Among those in attendance were
Tolima's Governor Eduardo Alzate Garcia,
Secretary Valencia, and area mayors. Plans
call for an initial government investment
of approximately $200,000 US dollars for
construction projects related to Armero.
Although the exact amount has not been set,
additional government financing will come
from the bonanza that Colombia has been
enjoying as a result of sharp increases
in international coffee prices. Colombia
is also applying for loans, totaling $300
million US dollars. The Inter-American
Development Bank and the World Bank already
have plans to provide a $34 million US
dollar loan.

It remains to be seen how quickly Colombian
officials can put together a comprehensive
planning package to help the thousands in
desperate need of housing, schools, and
jobs.

The role of the Church is difficult. It
can respond more quickly to the needs of

Debris on Armero Street.

the people, but lacks the financial clout wielded by the slower moving government. It is still mourning the dead, but must still provide comfort and support to the living, to ensure that survivors from Armero, like little Carmen Julia will have a future.

One figure who came to symbolize the tragedy more than any other was 13-year old Omayra Sanchez who suffered an indescribable fate. When the wave of mud hit she started out of her house, but stopped to try and help a sibling. She was trapped. For almost three days she was pinned helplessly from the waist down by the wreckage. Beneath her were the bodies of her father, grandmother, aunt, and cousin. Later, workers would discover that a concrete slab had trapped her. She was also clutched tight by the arms of her dead aunt. As the water kept rising around her, rescue workers lacked the equipment to save her as all efforts to free her from the debris that trapped her proved fruitless.

She became a symbol of Colombia's anguish. Television cameras focused on her as she endured her plight. The world watched in quiet desperation as she gave a rare display of courage and faith. She never panicked or screamed. Instead she sang songs for her rescuers and prayed for her family and friends. The day she died, she assured everyone, "Don't worry, God is waiting for me."

Tragically, just a couple of hours before her death, a pump arrived that would have enabled rescuers to drain the area around her and free her. But it was broken and proved useless. Just four hours later 18 more pumps arrived, but it was too late.

Her mother, a nurse named Maria Aleida was visiting Bogota at the time. She was stranded over a hundred miles away. When she first saw her daughter's plight it was a picture in a newspaper being read by another passenger on the bus she riding. She rushed to a TV as quickly as she could and watched her daughter's agony in horror.

Several months later my wife and I visited Maria where she was staying in an apartment in the south of Bogota. At first she didn't want to talk to us when we knocked on her door. She said she was tired of journalists and talking about what happened. Unsure what to do we just stood in the doorway and expressed our sympathy. She was still so overcome with grief we found ourselves listening as she sobbed and mourned the loss of her daughter.

Finally, she shrugged and stood slightly to the side of the door. We entered. The curtains were drawn and we sat on the couch in the subdued light and watched helplessly as she wept softy. I don't know how much time passed—the awkward silence probably made it seem longer than it was—before she began to speak softly.

As she spoke her voice gained volume and a quiet firmness as she said, "I have seen her a thousand times on TV. I can hear her voice and see her face pleading for salvation. My soul cries... I can only imagine how much she must have suffered during those fifty-six hours of being trapped alive in the mud and ruins of our life and our home. The dreams are gone..." Her unfocused eyes looked past us at what I can only assume was the vision of those desperate moments that took her daughter.

She went on to say how when Omayra was born she told her husband that she had dreams for her daughter. As the child grew, she recounted how she was full of questions about religion. She remembered her daughter asking her father that, if God lived in the church where they worshipped, why did they never see Him? Her father told the girl that He was a spirit.

At times Maria's speech was rambling and

incoherent. She seemed to be searching for an answer to her daughter's ultimate display of faith during her last hours. She wondered aloud how such an abstract concept must have been confusing to the young child. But she seemed to take comfort in the fact that Omayra must have fervently believed that even though she didn't see God at the end, He was there with her. I obviously will never know what shaped her final behavior, just as Omayra's mother was speculating in her efforts to find some closure. My only certainty is that anyone who saw Omayra's final hours will be forever haunted by the heart-wrenching event. I know I am.

Visiting the Victims & Survivors

My wife, Nydia, and I also spent time in Lerida talking to people about the event and the future. Lerida is the nearby town where many of those who survived the tragedy fled. One family we visited told us the story of their desperate fight for survival in the aftermath of the destruction of their town. It was a story of nothingness—no home, no food, no place to live, no work, no schools, and no hope—typical of the plight of Armero's few survivors.

When we arrived at the small house where they were staying with family, there were a total of 11 people living in the cramped space. They were polite and offered us something to eat. It was only after they served the meager bowls of a basic corn porridge type of dish, with no salt or seasoning of any kind, that we realized that was probably all they had. They were at once humble, yet, fiercely proud and independent. You could sense the dichotomy. They didn't want any charity, but they were desperate and looking for any hope.

As soon as we could during a break in the conversation, Nydia and I exchanged glances and asked if a couple of the older children might accompany us downtown, promising we would return as quickly as possible. They agreed. We set off in our Fiat station wagon to the nearest grocery store and filled the rear space to capacity with all manner of food staples, milk, fruit, and whatever else we saw, realizing it was a very temporary solution to a very permanent problem.

When we returned to the house, the family excitedly helped us unload. I particularly noted Pablo, the head of the family, with moist eyes as he thanked us. Later that day he asked me to walk with him. I did and in a barely auditable voice he expressed some of the quiet anger and rage that seemed to be buried deep within him.

He told me of the supplies, hundreds of tents, and other aid that had arrived in the area only to mysteriously disappear almost as fast as it was taken off trucks. (This coincided with some things my wife had seen with our own eyes: for example, truckloads of tents from the US that were there one day and gone the next.) As a reporter, he implored me to try and shed some light so that the truth would be known and force the authorities to do the right thing. I assured him I would do whatever I could.

I didn't have the heart to tell him that I had no powerful news organization supporting me. Like him, I was at the mercy of others. In my case I could only investigate and write. It was up to nameless editors to pick and choose what would see its way into print. Nonetheless, I was determined to do all I could.

Digging for Answers

Later that night, determined to honor his request, we headed back towards the department capital of Ibague. The following day, with Nydia's persistence, we were fortunate enough to get an interview with Governor Garcia. We settled into his downtown office and, and with Nydia translating, I started firing away.

I found him a combination of defensive and genuinely embarrassed. Here is part of that exchange after we got the niceties out of the way.

"Have you been surprised by the outpouring of the international community?"

"Yes, they have been very generous, especially Europe and the United States."

"Has most of it been in the form of financial aid or in other forms, such as medical equipment, tents, food, and that sort of thing?"

"Money from both governments and private organizations has come in, but that has gone to our federal government for administration and disbursement to us."

I pressed a little more. "How about the other forms of aid? Has that come directly into this area for your administration and disbursement?"

At this point it was obvious that he could see where this was going and he was visibly uncomfortable and tried to change the subject.

I continued, "We have visited Armero and surrounding communities, like Lerida, and I must confess I was a bit surprised when I didn't see more visible signs of the things we are talking about."

I then used the example of the tents my wife had seen shipped into the region and asked about what accountability measures he had in place.

"I can assure you that we are doing all we can with the resources at hand to provide support to the survivors."

I continued pressing, but after more than an hour I knew that was about as far as I was going to get. His answers became increasingly evasive and "politician" like. He tried to confuse the situation somewhat when he alluded to the fact that some of people themselves may have stolen some things owing to their desperate situation. He didn't, however, give any acknowledgement that officials may have been involved in stealing and selling items on the black market.

That night in our hotel room a few blocks away we were feeling a little paranoid. After all, reporters had disappeared for less. Although I must confess we had no tangible reason at that time to feel threatened. It was just an uncomfortable creepy feeling we had in the back of our minds. When we went out to eat dinner, we both found ourselves more than a little down and jumpy.

Nonetheless, we pondered what we could do next. I reminded my wife of what reconstruction President Gomez had said on national TV about his books being

The small city of Armero stood on the bleak plain shown.

open to all. I suggested maybe we should try a different approach and probe the money angle a bit.

For three days, and periodically for months thereafter, I tried to secure an interview with Gomez, but was unsuccessful. I talked to many secretaries and administrators, but was politely stonewalled at every attempt. To this day I don't know if Gomez was even aware of my attempts to interview him, but I suspect he was.

I took little solace in the fact that, to my knowledge, no one was ever tried or convicted for theft of aid resources as the result of any mainstream media investigative journalism—let alone as the result of any of my stories. This shook me and I was left feeling empty and hollow.

Climbing the Giant

Before we left the area around Armero to head back to our home in Pasto, there was one last thing we wanted to do. That was, climb the monster that had brought about all of these chaotic and tragic events. We headed towards the city of Manizales. Even from the distance, the base of Nevado del Ruiz was massive and intimidating, actually spanning the departments of Caldas, Quindio, and Tolima. It didn't matter that I estimated it would take several days to drive around it because we wanted to drive up it.

Access to the volcano was still closed to the public because of periodic volcanic activity, which made Nydia and me all the more nervous and excited. We drove through the spectacular mountains and switchbacks. Dusk settled in around us and I noticed the gas gauge in our Fiat getting low, but I calculated that we had sufficient fuel and we pressed on. The paved road eventually gave way to dirt as the car's little engine strained up the increasingly steep slope. We passed a sign for the Refugio del Ruiz—a popular lodge high on the side of the volcano. In the fading light we could see large rocks and boulders strewn about the landscape. We assumed these were from the blast that had swept Armero away.

The higher we went, the more clouds closed in around us like a dense fog. Even with our headlights on, we could barely see ten feet ahead. At that point the car literally gasped to take in enough air for the engine to function. (It is impossible to say with any precision, but I estimate we were over 12,000 feet up the volcano.) We realized that even if we were able to go higher it would be too dark to take any photographs.

In one of the most harrowing moments of the trip we found ourselves headed up a sharp incline enclosed in a fog-like cocoon. I stopped and put on the emergency brake to keep from rolling back. My wife's relief that I was going to turn around and head down was short lived when we both realized that all we could see was a murky view of the narrow dirt track. We had no way of knowing if the edge dropped off to nothingness. Cautiously, I worked the emergency brake, gas, and manual transmission to maneuver around to get us headed back down. It was a slow process as I jockeyed the car around, afraid to get too close to the edge. By that time we were in total darkness. Finally as we started to roll back down, my wife looked at me and told me good naturedly how crazy I was. I acknowledged the fact that I might have been a bit driven, but I really needed the photos to use and sell to European and US media outlets.

We stopped talking about our gas situation, but it was plainly on both of our minds. At the turn off to the Refuge I stopped and said I thought we should spend the night there, not mentioning that I was fairly certain we didn't have enough gas to get back to civilization. We agreed and headed toward what we hoped would truly be a refuge for us.

It turned out to be a long two story yellow building. We approached the large lodge and the empty parking lot. Complete darkness confirmed our unspoken fear that it was closed, abandoned. Nonetheless, we pulled up to the front door, got out, and knocked loudly. It was a scene from a horror movie and my imagination was running wild. I don't know what my wife was thinking, but it couldn't have been comforting thoughts. We peered through the windows. At first I couldn't be sure, but then I saw the weak flicker of light from within the building. It slowly grew brighter.

The door opened and a man and a woman peered out from behind a candle, giving their expressions a ghostly appearance. It turned out they were the caretakers. We introduced ourselves and explained what we were doing there. They said the hotel was closed because of the danger of further eruptions and the fact that there was no electricity. I explained that we needed lodging and I was worried about running out of gas.

They were kind and beyond gracious. The invited us in and we all went to the huge dining room where they

On our climb up. Water stream running through lava.

set up more candles. The woman then offered us food
and drink, which we gratefully accepted. The four of us

sat there in the huge dining room and ate by candlelight and talked about the disaster. They suggested that we take a dip in the large pool fed by hot springs that was located at the end of the dining hall behind a glass enclosure. The air was heavy with the smell of sulfur, but it wasn't unpleasant.

The man helped me bring in our bags from the car. Nydia and I changed into shorts and plunged into the water. It was surreal. Mist rose off the surface as we paddled around while they sat at the edge of the pool and we talked more. They explained that the hotel was famous for its spring fed hot, healing, sulfur waters. In addition, they said Colombians liked to ski there since it was situated at the edge of the perpetual snow pack that crowned the volcano.

They not only insisted that we stay the night, but also said they would send for a guide to accompany us to the summit of the volcano. They warned that we would have to set off before daybreak and be at the top by the time the sun rose because it was only clear for an hour or two in the morning. After that, the clouds moved in and blocked any vista.

We were exhausted and our hosts showed us to our room. The solitude of the hotel was startling and spooky as we walked down long dark corridors holding a candelabra to light the way. The air was cold and still. Once in our room we decided to sleep in our clothes to keep warm and to be prepared in the event that the volcano rumbled again. We lay in the darkness and wondered how the building had been spared getting hit by the large rocks that must have crashed down, which we had seen littering the landscape outside.

We drifted off to sleep. It was dark and still when they knocked on our door at 4:30 in the morning. We splashed some cold water on our faces from an old fashioned ceramic water basin and met them in the dining hall. They had laid out wool ponchos and heavy jackets for us since the clothes we had worn in the warm valley below were totally inadequate for ascending to 18,000 feet. They also had prepared a stack of arepas— round, flat corn meal food stuffed with cheese, which they wrapped in a cotton towel. In addition, they had a container of hot chocolate and a flask of aquardiente to ward off the cold.

As we bundled into our borrowed clothes our guide showed up. I liked him immediately. His native features were set in an almost Zen like expression. He was short, powerfully built and seemed to radiate a calm confidence. We climbed back into the Fiat as our hosts stood there and wished us luck. In the dawn the yellow lodge looked like a scene from Switzerland.

As I started the engine, I noticed that the gas gauge registered more fuel than I remembered. I looked at our host and, as if reading my mind, he smiled and told me he had a can of gas which he had taken the liberty of putting in the tank. At this point I knew I was having more good fortune than I had a right to expect.

With confidence we set off, my wife and I in front

and our guide sitting calmly in the backseat. The dirt track didn't seem so threatening in the slowly emerging daylight. The little car struggled higher and higher as the landscape started to resemble an otherworldly moonscape. At one point it sputtered and could go no further.

I looked back at our guide. He said we were close and could go the last distance on foot. We abandoned the car and set off. The air was invigorating, but thin, causing us to struggle to breathe. The cold was sharp to the point that it seemed to penetrate our bones. We were grateful for the foresight of the wonderful couple from the hotel as we enjoyed a few swigs of the strong liquor and munched on arepas.

After a trek, we made it to the summit. You could see where a large portion of the peak had been blown away during the eruption. Wisps of mist, clouds, and smoke swirled around, giving us glimpses of surrounding countryside for miles below. You could physically feel the power of the volcano, its sheer imposing size overwhelming any sense of proportion. We stood there in silence, the only sound being the soft mournful whine of the wind, contemplating how anything so surreally beautiful could be so deadly.

The sun had just turned the dawn to day, but we could already see the clouds starting to form over the mighty mountain. Even though it's located close to the equator, its sheer altitude makes the air frigid. In spite of our heavy clothing, in less than an hour we were

Nevado del Ruiz shrouded by clouds and smoke in the far distance.

thoroughly numb.

As we descended, the moonscape took on an English moor look like something out of a Sherlock Holmes film, the coarse vegetation creating pastel shades of pink, purple, and a pale green. The land was at once desolate, yet alive, giving it an outer space quality.

Since our guide had been so quiet throughout the morning, I was surprised when he described how this area was often subject to strong hailstorms. He said it covered everything in ice for brief periods until the sun regained control and burned it off. It was hard to imagine what an ice storm there would look like because that day the sun flooded the landscape in intermittent bursts—the mist and clouds giving the whole scene a mysterious quality.

We stopped back at the Refuge to change clothes and thank our hosts again. Then, humbled by their generosity, the spirit of Armero's survivors, and the volcano, we headed home to Pasto over a thousand kilometers away.

5

The Explosive Treasures of Tumaco

One of the best kept secrets at that time was the Pacific coast of Colombia. I traveled there many times when I lived in Pasto as the region was just starting to show signs of realizing its potential. From the time I arrived in the capital of Nariño, I had heard what a spectacular transition it was from the mountain city to the ocean.

From Pasto, at over 8,000 feet, you head down the long slope of the Andes range to sea level over a distance of 180 miles. I was told that the road, though, was mostly unpaved and a trip by car could take over 10 hours.

I learned later that you descend through a region of rain forests. One part called "La Planada" is managed by a Colombian couple. They have a main house and dormitories where scientists from all over the world come to study the incredible variety of plant and animal life.

This incredible array of nature ranges from literally dozens of types of orchids and large vampire bats to recently discovered species of frogs with translucent bodies that enable you to see their hearts and other organs. It is also home to the Oso con gafas, a black bear with light-colored markings around its eyes that make it look like it's wearing eyeglasses.

Morning mist burns off at La Planada. The peaks are a series of volcanoes, including Nevado de Cumbal, in the distance. The main house is just visible in the lower left corner.

Once you pass through the rainy jungle you start to see a staggering array of trees, ranging from teak to mahogany and more. Based on this plethora of wood, the Colombians had even built a plywood factory in partnership with Japan and the US. The plan was to export the finished product to Asia.

The main city, Tumaco, itself is unique. In addition to such commodities as wood and shrimp, it's also the gateway for the export of oil from the southern part of the country via the 190 mile long Transandino pipeline. It terminates at the small port city where pumping stations transport the crude oil to waiting tankers offshore.

Not surprisingly, this petroleum distribution point had become a tempting target for rebels. I wondered at the time if there might be a story there, but had no idea how I might go about pursuing it. All I knew was that guerrillas routinely sought to sabotage the Transandino. Besides the fact that the pipeline runs through a vast jungle region, I also knew that they sometimes planted landmines in the area after attacking the pipeline, making it even more difficult for authorities to repair the damage. The thought of such a story stuck in the back of my mind and I filed it away.

It wasn't long before I planned my first road trip to the Pacific coast. It was overcast the day Armando Gutierrez and I set off. He was a friend and neighbor and often served as my translator for stories when my wife couldn't accompany me. He was tall—perhaps six feet—with a moderately heavy build. His unflappable demeanor had served both of us well in some unusual situations.

By the time we actually got on the road it was late afternoon, making the cloudy day even darker. After we left Pasto the paved road soon gave way to a rutted dirt track, made muddy by recent rains. Armando was driving his car and we bounced along doing our best to avoid the deepest potholes and ruts in the road. As we drove he described various areas along the way. One was a trail which angled off the main road that he told me went to a tiny pueblo a few kilometers into the lush vegetation. He knew of it because friends of his were mining for gold there.

It was before midnight when Armando muttered something a few seconds before I sensed something wrong with the car.

Then he said, "We have a flat tire and we have no spare."

I glanced nervously out into the darkness and wondered what we would do. He was serious, but didn't seem too concerned. I was afraid to ask so I waited for him to say something as we bumped slowly along in the black night on the dirt road on the deflated tire. In the periphery of our headlights, dark vegetation formed shapes and shadows on the sides of the road as we limped along.

He must have sensed my thoughts and said, "Don't worry, we will get it fixed."

I couldn't resist and said, "You must be joking. Where?"

He just grinned and gripped the wheel.

As if by magic we spotted the glow of weak lights in the distance. It wasn't even a town, just a collection of a few basic houses made of adobe with thatched roofs. They seemed to be illuminated by lamps or candles and I realized there was no electricity. This should be interesting, I thought.

In front of one house, with the flicker of light spilling out the front windows, I could see a pole about three meters high. What appeared to be a tire was mounted on the top. We bumped to a halt.

A friendly man appeared in the doorway, carrying a lantern. He was short and slender. He wore some type of dark cotton pants, a stained short sleeved white shirt, and sandals. I saw a curtain flutter and briefly glimpsed the face of a child.

Armando pointed to the tire and they exchanged greetings. Unfazed the man said something I couldn't understand and disappeared around the back of the one or two room house. He returned carrying a jack and some tools.

Before I could ask Armando how in the world he was going to patch the tire, he motioned for me to be patient. I watched as the wiry man jacked up the car, removed the tire, and placed it flat on the ground. Then with great skill he manipulated two pry bars by positioning and hopping on them until the tire popped off the rim. He ran his hand inside and found the protrusion of a large nail, which he removed and proudly showed us. All of this was done by the glow of the lantern.

Next he removed the tube and using a large bellows type hand air pump (actually operated with his foot) inflated the tube enough to determine where the hole was located. Using a small rasp, he roughed up the surface around it.

Then he produced a small, flat, oval shaped aluminum disk. As he peeled back a strip of paper I could see a thin rubber layer on the metal. He stuck the disk over the hole and pressed. Satisfied, he pulled a box of wooden matches from his pocket, handed them to Armando and motioned for him to strike one. I watched as he lit the backside of the metal disk. The tire man let it flare for a few seconds then blew the flame out. Afterwards he pried off the metal disk. What was left was a perfect patch.

His skill was impressive. He glanced at me, grinned, and said, "Vulcanize."

I had heard the term as a kid in connection with tires or tire making, I couldn't recall exactly, but realized that the term had taken on a whole other meaning.

Just as skillfully he stuffed the tube into the tire, remounted it on the rim, and inflated it. I shook my head as he placed the tire on the car. Armando paid him and with that we were on our way. I remember thinking of the pneumatic tools and hydraulic presses used in gas stations in the US. This man had produced the same results. No power. No problem.

I had many such trips to the coast and each one fascinated me. As I slowly became familiar with the forces at work in the area, I realized that both its potential and remoteness had made it the focus for those who wanted investments and tangible progress the traditional way versus those who saw it as an opportunity to change the system.

Every time I left Tumaco I wondered who would ultimately change it—those with a gun or those with dreams of building an economic powerhouse. After all, both had their agendas, even though they were diametrically opposed.

This moved me to increasingly seek stories that went beyond feature articles for magazines and newspapers and to focus more on investigative journalism. As far as I could tell major publications like El Tiempo, the big daily newspaper based out of the capital, had not ventured much into this part of Colombia.

Unfortunately, it turned out that I stumbled into a few situations that I neither fully understood nor was fully equipped to handle without the support of an established news organization.

The story set forth below epitomizes (at least to me) my foray into the hidden world of insurgency and violence against the establishment. It centers on efforts to cause problems for the State by disrupting the transport of oil from the fields to Tumaco via the Transandino pipeline to tankers anchored off the coast.

A Shot in the Dark

Tumaco, Nariño, Colombia
July 1986

I was always struck by the unique qualities that

defined Tumaco. Qualities I could sense even with my eyes closed. This trip was no different. The humid air filled with the cloying scent of decaying vegetation mingled with the faint odor of salty sea air and wood smoke. Oddly enough, the area also awakened a primal sense in me. From the moment I entered the region I had the feeling of being watched. It was ever present and always lurking in the back of my mind. No matter how I tried to dismiss it, every instinct told me I was the subject of unseen eyes. I always felt it deep in my gut. It was like a shadow flitting across my unconscious thoughts.

On this particular trip we planned to stay for several days. Armando and I were discussing how we might go about getting a hard news story about the spate of oil pipeline bombings. He was highly motivated because as my translator his fortunes were tied to mine. If he helped with a solid story and I sold it, then we both got paid. When my wife wasn't translating for me, I relied on him because although my Spanish was passable, he had proved invaluable at both facilitating conversations and story translations for publications like the big Colombian dailies El Espectador and La Republica.

From what I had read the acts of terrorism and threats of bombings were being attributed to leftist rebels. (Discussed in more detail in Chapter 7 on guerrillas.) We had studied a map of the area and tried to discern a pattern of attacks. Armando had also begun to discretely ask around to see if any of the locals knew anything firsthand about these activities.

Finally, one morning after a late breakfast, he said he would be back later and promptly disappeared for two hours. When he returned he was in good spirits, informing me that this might be our lucky day. I asked why and he replied that we would go out later and he would show me. I was excited and wanted to know more, but he simply said we might have a lead but that he was not sure.

I thought we had reached a dead end when he received a phone call later in the day, after which he hung up and seemed thoughtful and disappointed. I asked for details and he said maybe things would be a go within the next day or two. We ate an early dinner, had a few drinks, and retired to our hotel.

The next day started unremarkably. Later that afternoon, though, he received another call and instantly became excited. He took me to a bar at the lower end of the dirt main street in our quest. As we walked on the wide, muddy road he told me our destination was a hangout for thieves, smugglers, and suspected guerrillas.

Once there, he quietly asked me to give him a fair amount of pesos, which he then passed discretely to the bartender who was a skinny, clean shaven chap with slicked back black hair. (Over the preceding months I had grown a full beard in my efforts to blend in under such situations as I now found myself. I was feeling quite confident that I appeared to be a subtle part of the whole scene.)

We ordered a favorite local drink called "refajo," which is a mixture of beer and Colombiana, an apple flavored soft drink. We sauntered over to a table and settled in.

The evening is etched into my mind. It was getting dark when Armando nudged me and tilted his head slightly forward. I followed his eyes to the bartender in time to see him nod his head in the direction of the door as two men entered. Armando told me to wait, grabbed our glasses and approached the bar under the guise of getting us more drinks. After several minutes of hushed conversation, I saw the bartender slide something toward Armando, which he palmed and slid into his pocket.

When he returned to the table I asked him what that was all about. "Transportation," he replied.

After another hour, the two men we had been casually observing were joined by another man. There was nothing especially distinguishing or remarkable about any of them. Two sported thick mustaches. They were all dressed in jeans and dark colored shirts. One wore a tattered navy blue baseball cap perched on the back of his head. I remember the hat because it had a Detroit Tigers baseball team emblem on it—one of my favorites. He seemed to be the leader based on the fact that the other men constantly looked at him. Unlike his companions his eyes continually scanned the room. When they passed over us there was no indication that he found us either threatening or even interesting. (So much for me thinking I looked sort of like a badass with my beard, black jeans, and boots.)

More time passed, probably about a half hour, before the trio left the bar together. We also paid our tab and left. By the time we were outside, they were climbing into a Jeep parked down the street. Armando turned the opposite direction. I followed him to a faded pale blue Land Rover. The ancient Rover looked like something you see on a National Geographic channel on safari in Africa—complete with a huge spare tire bolted to the hood. (It has stuck in my mind all these years because one of my brothers-in-law had one very similar, except that it was green. They were quite common in the country at that time.)

He fired it up and it was surprisingly quiet. As we sat there idling, I asked him how sure he was that those were our guys.

"I don't know," he said, "but that's what our guy says."

At that moment we shared the same thought that we had nothing to lose. Or, at least that's what we thought.

He pulled out behind them as they passed, letting them open up a block lead on us. They headed out of town and we bounced along behind them at a respectful distance. When our quarry was out of sight over a rise in the road, Armando switched off our headlights. The Rover squeaked and rocked along for nearly half an hour. We said little, each of us lost in our thoughts.

At some point we realized that their taillights were no longer visible and I lamented that we had lost them. Armando braked and began to back up slowly. After several minutes we saw it. Off to our right was a muddy lane that had been hacked into the thick vegetation. We turned into it and proceeded at a snail's pace.

Growing up around guns in southern Arizona, I knew immediately that the series of sharp cracks were the reports of rifle shots. I exchanged glances with Armando as he braked and pushed off the muddy track as far as possible.

He asked if I wanted to turn back. His words seemed barely audible over the pounding of my chest, but I heard myself saying I wanted to go ahead on foot, telling him that we came here to hopefully get some pictures and whatever information we could gather and I wanted to try. (Ironically, looking back later I realized that in my excitement I had failed to even record the license plate number of the vehicle we had been trailing.)

I really wanted to break a hard news story and tried to prepare accordingly. Back at the hotel earlier in the day I had loaded my camera with the fastest film I had—which I believe was ISO 2000—and I hoped I could get something in the low light. I had preset the shutter, aperture, and other settings in preparation of having to operate in near darkness.

We got out of the Rover, leaving the doors ajar rather than risk the noise of closing them. Across the hood I could just make out a smile as Armando shook his head and said, "This is fucking crazy."

That line in itself was memorable because I had never heard him use such colorful or profane language. In fact, I didn't ever remember hearing him curse.

Our dark clothing blended into our surroundings. In addition, I had on a dark green vest stuffed with extra film, a light meter, and other photography tools. Over that was slung my camera bag.

He was barely visible, but I saw him motion forward. We moved slowly, stumbling along in the darkness. After a few minutes we could see vehicle taillights ahead. I recognized them as the Jeep we had been following.

We stopped and stood very still. Men were talking in low tones, their voices carrying on the thick air. Without warning, headlights from another vehicle parked in the opposite direction were switched on. Fortunately for us they were partially blocked by the Jeep and didn't penetrate our position. Instinctively we both stepped back a few paces.

I couldn't tell how many men there were, but from the shadows in the lights it appeared to be five or six. As we watched they slipped into the thick vegetation, leaving two behind. I could see one cradling a rifle and the other with his weapon slung over his shoulder.

We stood like statues, frozen in place as I reminded myself to breathe. I suspect Armando was thinking similar thoughts. I had no idea of what to do next. Obviously neither of us had thought that far ahead or planned what we might do given such a scenario.

One thing was sure. I was worried that leaving our Rover on the side of the road would cause big problems

A road cut through Tumaco's lush vegetation.

if one of the vehicles passed that way for whatever reason. Earlier I had gone over in my mind what I imagined would happen. I envisioned following them and then laying in wait from some hidden perch and shooting some fantastic photos that I could sell to a newspaper or magazine. At that minute, though, I knew such thinking may have been overly optimistic, if not just plain stupid.

One repeated thought that lurked in the back of my mind and kept flickering through my thoughts was that no one even knew where we were. If something happened, would they even know who we were since neither of us was carrying any identification? My passport was with the local law enforcement.

By this time, the creatures of the night had found us. I could sense and feel what I assumed were mosquitoes zeroing in on my face, neck and arms. They sounded like deadly tiny helicopters as they buzzed in to insert their painful little lances into my flesh. I waved my arms defensively and wished I could light a cigarette and drive them off with smoke.

I quietly crossed the road and whispered to Armando. "What do you think?"

Visions of my wife and our two innocent little girls were definitely coloring my thoughts. Actually, my wife had no idea where I was. No one did. We stood there in silence for a few moments thinking about possible moves we could make, none of them with good outcomes. I mentally cursed myself for a lack of planning and preparation, in general, and a failure to think things through.

As it turned out, things quickly changed to nudge us off dead center when a loud explosion sent us to the ground. Then a few seconds of silence. That ended with the sound of gunfire and men yelling. We could hear what sounded like heavy vehicles approaching from the opposite direction.

That was enough. In unspoken communication we both scrambled to our feet and began running back to the Rover, my bulky camera bag banging uncomfortably against my side. Gasping for air, we clamored into the relative safety of the cab. Mercifully, the engine of the big machine caught on the first crank.

Armando jockeyed the Rover around in a series of three point turns on the greasy surface. At one point we slipped too far off the road and all four tires were spinning as the Rover rocked and fought for traction. I remember talking to it as though it was a horse pulling a wagon, urging it forward. "Come on baby," played in an endless loop in my mind. Finally free and pointed in the right direction, we raced as fast as possible back to the main road and headed for town.

I lit two cigarettes and handed one to Armando with trembling hands. The smoke we exhaled punctuated our nervous laughter as we started to congratulate ourselves. Although looking back, for the life of me I am unsure what we were celebrating. We had accomplished nothing other than getting our hearts racing.

Our relief, however, was short lived. As we rounded a turn we saw military vehicles flanking a wooden barricade. I remember cursing in my best sailor language and Armando muttering under his breath. We coasted to a halt as men in fatigues approached. My heart sank as one of my favorite police officers emerged from the peripheral darkness.

I must take a slight pause here and recount my prior encounter with the good policeman to put into context my relationship with him. It started a few months before when Armando and I had booked a double room at the little hotel we often used. It was a simple room with two twin beds and a bathroom with a shower. Laying in bed you could see the front wall. It featured tall narrow windows with wooden shutters and moveable slats. Even when closed they allowed light to enter from Tumaco's main street two stories below.

A few days after our arrival, a commotion in our room woke me in the small hours of the night. As my eyes adjusted to the light I could see figures silhouetted against the windows. How many I didn't know, but they appeared to be in uniform and carried weapons. A lamp was switched on and I noticed that the group of men was clustered around my bed, not Armando's.

At first, I experienced an all too familiar feeling. That is, I believed I was being kidnapped. The thought as usual was terrifying. By this time Armando was awake. In Spanish he asked who they were and what they wanted. The cop didn't answer immediately. He simply pushed through his men, pulled a chair to the edge of my bed, brushed my clothes off it onto the floor, and sat down. I was still lying flat, elevated a bit by my elbows. I started to get up, but he motioned for me to stay where I was.

Again Armando asked what was going on. The officer began asking questions in Spanish. His voice had an edge but he seemed patient. His eyes never left me, even though Armando was doing the answering.

The gist was that when foreigners checked into a hotel they were required to leave their passports with reception. These were then passed to the local police to monitor those moving through the region.

In our case, I had never given the owner and his wife my passport. I had a healthy paranoia about letting it out of my possession. The proprietors understood and had never insisted. It was as simple as that, but the officer was insinuating that my reasons were more sinister and he was insisting to know who I was and why I was there.

Armando tried to explain and we quickly reached an impasse. We all sat there in silence for a few minutes, the cop studying me and his men standing there with their weapons trained in my direction. Finally with an exasperated shrug he asked for my passport.

I gestured toward my camera bag and he motioned for one of the men to retrieve it. After rifling through it he pulled out the familiar blue jacket and studied it. When he flipped to the page with my resident visa, he smiled cynically and abruptly switched to passable English.

He asked me the question I had heard a thousand times—did I work for the CIA. As always when asked, I tried to look amused and said I didn't work for any American government organization. To say he looked skeptical would be an understatement. Next he asked me if I honestly expected him to believe that.

Now it was my turn to shrug and advise him to believe what he would but that was the truth.

He pushed himself up then leaned close to my face and told me they took their laws seriously and advised me to be very careful. This was accentuated by a wagging of his finger as he repeated the being careful part.

I told him I wanted my passport back and he informed me that he would relinquish it when I was leaving Tumaco. I had to settle for that. He left the room and his men followed as abruptly as they had entered, leaving the door wide open. Armando and I exchanged glances.

That was the beginning of my brief and somewhat odd relationship with the man.

After emerging from the shadows that night, he eyed both Armando and me for a long moment. Then he proceeded to walk slowly around the Rover with a flashlight. I was sure the fact that it was caked with fresh, thick mud didn't escape his attention.

He approached the driver's side and played his flashlight in front of our faces. Blinded I felt him studying me during the uncomfortable silence.

When he spoke he simply asked why he was not surprised to see me. I remained silent, unsure of what to say and unwilling to dig my awkward hole any deeper.

Men who have experienced war describe a certain scent of fear—a mixture of stale sweat and something indefinable, perhaps a musky odor. I smelled it at that moment. It seemed to fill the Rover. The officer nodded his head and one of his men swung the barricade away.

I was told to get out and was replaced by a policeman with a machine pistol. He then informed me to ride with him and Armando could follow.

With a sense of dread I climbed into the back of his Jeep. The driver revved it up and we started back towards Tumaco. Visions of a jail cell danced though my mind and I wondered if I would be allowed to call the embassy in Bogota.

Our conversation, though tense, was civil enough on the ride back. I attempted to recreate it as faithfully as possible later that day when I recorded it in my journal. It went something like this, starting with the now familiar question.

"Who are you really?"

"A reporter."

"Who do you work for?"

"Myself."

"You are a reporter with no newspaper. Is that what

I am supposed to believe? Interesting."

I could hear the sarcasm in his voice even though he was speaking in halting English.

"It's the truth."

I tried to elaborate that I was a freelancer. He said he didn't understand. Next I tried saying I was a stringer for a news syndicate out of Chicago. Again, I knew my story sounded somewhat unbelievable, even to my ears.

"I doubt it. Are you CIA?" he pushed.

Still I persisted. "Not hardly."

"I could check with your embassy in Bogota, but what would be the point? They would undoubtedly lie for you."

I saw some hope and said, "Please do check with them. They won't lie to you. They will verify what I am saying. I have nothing to hide."

Before I could stop him he grabbed my camera bag and removed a map tucked in a side pocket. He flipped on his flashlight and studied it. I saw his finger trace the highlighted path of the TransAndino pipeline. He gave me an inquisitive look.

"You have an interest in oil?"

"Not really," I replied.

"Then what were you doing out there?" Sightseeing?

"Driving."

He shook the map, clearly frustrated. He then asked if I saw him as a joke, just a stupid country policeman.

I said not at all, but he seemed unconvinced.

As a foreigner, I had really been working on trying

to put myself in the shoes of others. At that point, I wondered what I would do with me if I were him. It was then that I clearly realized that he was just trying to do his job. I also realized that would be made easier if I showed him some obvious respect. Moreover, I really had nothing to hide. So, I decided to use a different approach to deal with him.

With a new tone, punctuated with "señor," I launched into my story, following the truth as closely as I dared without raising even more doubts and questions or calling attention to my ineffectiveness in pursuing a situation I was clearly not equipped to deal with. I used a mixture of English and Spanish, leaving out the name of the bar and the bartender.

To his credit he listened patiently.

As I ended my tale, he asked, "Do you realize how stupid all of this sounds?"

I remained silent and just nodded in agreement. There followed an uncomfortably long silence. He seemed to be wrestling with a decision. Finally, he barked some words at the driver. I was more than a little surprised when a few minutes later we pulled up in front of the hotel.

Not really believing my good fortune I just sat there. He twisted in his seat and stared at me, his features barely visible in the glow of the street lights. "I have decided that you are either a bobo (fool or idiot in Spanish) or really who you say you are."

He didn't push me further or ask for details to

clarify some central points of my story. He simply said, "Perhaps you should be a policeman. You don't seem to be very good at reporting."

That hurt a little. I didn't agree about the reporting part and knew I wouldn't be a good policeman, but I wasn't about to argue.

At that point I saw the first smile I had ever seen on his face. "Go. Get out of here and don't overstay your welcome."

I nodded with gratitude and climbed out. I resisted the urge to keep talking and told myself to just shut up. I couldn't believe it was over. I was disappointed, but immensely relieved. I noticed that the vehicle following with Armando was parked behind us. He was as clearly confused and relieved as I was.

The realization hit me that we had a story of sorts, but not the story I had hoped for. I have recounted that night, though, because it captures the feeling in Colombia in the wild 1980s—a place where powerful forces were at work to fulfill the country's promise and to address its contradictions. The drug cartels, the guerrillas, and the government of that era all clashing and aligning, creating an environment that was at once unpredictable and often dangerous.

In some intangible, but discernible way the conditions of the time seemed to permeate the very atmosphere everywhere I went. You could actually sense it in the air. After all, the rebels controlled approximately 50 percent of Colombia at the time.

I was shocked the next afternoon when I returned from lunch with Armando and saw the policeman again. This time he was lounging in the lobby in civilian clothing, reading a newspaper.

He stood when he saw me. Seeing the worry on my face he quickly said, "Don't worry. I'm not here in an official capacity. You like aquardiente?[4]"

The question completely threw me and I nodded dumbly. He dismissed Armando with a wave and we left the hotel trailed by a couple of men in uniform. A short walk and we ensconced ourselves in a bar about a block down the street from the hotel. For two hours we drank and talked.

One of my burning questions was what had happened the night before since there was no mention of gunfire or the explosion in the local media. He just smiled and shrugged, deflecting the question by saying, "It does not concern you in any way. Leave it alone." Then he would steer the conversation back to more personal matters.

(I never found out what really happened that night. It remains a complete mystery to me. Periodically I searched the media out of curiosity, and while I found accounts of guerrilla attacks on the pipeline, I never found mention of this particular event. Since the pipeline wasn't damaged that night, I can only speculate that somehow the attempt was foiled and that the explosives were set off prematurely in some struggle between the

---

4   An extremely popular anise-flavored Colombian liquor that is very strong.

authorities and the rebels.)

At first I wondered if the invitation to share a few drinks was a trick to get me to open up, but then decided I was being too much of a cynic and his gesture was genuine.

We chatted amicably and I learned he had two young sons. I talked about my family. Our drinking bout was an enjoyable surprise, but his ability to do the unexpected didn't end there.

He finally stood and informed me he had to go. Before he left he casually flipped my passport on the table. "You are leaving and I would advise you to plan better if you return."

I asked if I could have a couple of days to wrap up a story I had been working on and he shrugged noncommittally.

(My casual attempts in the past few years to locate and contact him drew more suspicion than information and I decided not pursue the matter further. Instead I am left to speculate on his fate. In actuality, I regret not making a better effort to stay in contact with him. I believe he was a good man with a hard job during a difficult time.)

Back to Basics

So, for that moment it was back to features. Something I seemed to do best. Fortunately, I had received an assignment from the Organization of American States—the official economic, political, cultural, and military alliance of all South American countries. Headquartered in Washington, DC, the OAS is a powerful voice for South America. The following is the story I filed for them.

Tapping the Treasures of Tumaco[5]

Pasto, the lofty capital of the department of Nariño, sits in the shadow of the Galeras Volcano. From its cold peak, on a clear day, you can see over 180 miles across a tropical belt to the Pacific Ocean. With its rich natural resources, many people believe it is a view of the future.

Nariño's port of Tumaco is the economic center for this coastal lowland of endless summer, whose seasons are marked only by the amount of rainfall. Exotic woods and fruits are plentiful. It is the site of one of the largest palm oil plantations in South America. There are long stretches of sparkling unspoiled beaches. The waters teem with marine life, and experts say that offshore banks provide some of the best fishing grounds in the world.

Even with such a vast array of natural resources, the region remains largely

---

5   Excerpted from Tapping the Treasures of Tumaco by Michael F. Kastre, which appeared in Las Americas, the official magazine of the Organization of American States (OAS), September-October 1986.

isolated and undeveloped. Since there are no buildings over four stories tall, the city of 45,000 has no recognizable skyline. Most structures are made of wood. There are few modern buildings or cement sidewalks, and the unpaved streets are dusty on dry days and become muddy with sudden rains. There is a vibrant undercurrent, but the potential of Tumaco has yet to be realized. A group of business and civic leaders is changing this, though.

The centerpiece of Tumaco's economic development is the production of oil from African palms (known as oil palms in many parts of the world). Currently there are over 18,000 acres in production in the region, almost half with the giant Palmas de Tumaco. With its 1,000 workers, the plantation has created a social entity within the community. Their new processing plant is not the largest, but is capable of producing 30 tons of oil per hour and it is the most modern in South America.

It takes the hardy palms four to five years to bear fruit, but the wait is worthwhile. After five years they will produce over a ton of fruit per acre. This increases to 5 tons per year when the trees are 10 years old. Twenty percent of the fruit is oil, which is used in such products as margarine, cooking oil, and cosmetics.

Typical of Tumaco's new breed of farmer is Carlos Alberto Corredor of the Hacienda Paleiras Plantation. Educated in the United States, he returned to Colombia to put his knowledge to work. According to Corredor, "In many areas we are ready for high technology, although often its application is not necessary. Basic technology goes a long way. For example, a small investment in fertilizer often can increase yield three or four times. The difficult part is convincing people that while it's true that the investment in technology costs money now, it will pay off later. It's a matter of getting people to keep an open mind and rethink old ways."

The surrounding region also offers opportunity for small landowners with limited funds and access to technology. Over 400 campesinos (country folks) have organized the Cooperativa de Palmicultores de Tumaco (Palm Farmer's Cooperative of Tumaco). Known as Coopalmaco, they have almost 25,000 acres of mature, virgin wood. German Manzi, accountant for Coopalmaco and the Chamber of Commerce, said, "Sixty-eight different species of commercial wood have been identified. The plan is to harvest 120 acres at a time. Once the wood is cut and sold, the land will be replanted with African palms." When completed, the co-op could produce over 20,000 tons of palm oil annually.

Others are trying to bring the wealth of the ocean to the fertile land. At present, 95 percent of the world shrimp production comes from the sea, but the increasingly high cost of operating ships makes this method less attractive each year. The land surrounding Tumaco could support some 120,000 acres of shrimp production once large shallow ponds are built, flooded with seawater, and stocked with shrimp larvae.

Colombian shrimp expert Marcial Gardeazabel noted that one acre could produce 800 pounds of shrimp per year. He observed, "At a price of $5 per pound it's easy to see what the impact could be. In 10 years this could generate 10,000 new jobs, and 90 percent would be for unskilled workers, because cleaning shrimp does not lend itself to automation."

Shrimp farmer Alfredo Willis said, "Tumaco is one of the very few places in the world that has the ideal conditions for producing shrimp in a controlled environment. The water and air temperatures are perfect. We are in the process of building a shrimp farm by combining high technology with available materials. For instance, our initial 20 acre pond will have a wood gate instead of concrete, but the pumping station will be state-of-the-art. We feel this type of approach offers the best future for the small producer because it is less costly."

Belgian-born Chris Van Saene is building a farm for growing shrimp larvae. He has completed four tanks, but said, "I need a total of 36 to be able to produce a sufficient amount of larvae." His Acquacultura Matilde company will supply shrimp farms with high quality larvae to stock the ponds.

According to Van Saene, "You can get larvae from pools that flood in from the ocean, but in the massive quantities required, you need to grow them. It's a tricky business because the larvae need special food to get started. I will have tanks to grow plankton, algae, and other foods, as well as tanks for the shrimp themselves. Special systems are required to circulate the water and keep the food suspended. If this is not done, it settles to the bottom and causes problems."

Until this part of the industry is fully

established, it may be the limiting factor
to creating the giant business many people
envision. Tumaco has less than 125 acres of
shrimp ponds in actual operation, but many
more are scheduled to begin operation this
year. Plans call for production to be 20,000
pounds per year in 5 years, increasing to
a whopping 60,000 pounds within 10 years.

Colombia is the only South American
country that fronts both oceans, making
it a natural gateway to world and domestic
markets. But reaching these ambitious
goals will not be easy. "We have a history
of isolation," explained Tumaco's mayor,
Ernesto Kaiser. "The only road from Tumaco
to the department capital of Pasto is
essentially unpaved. The 180 miles takes
12 hours of hard driving."

He is working hard to change this. Over 60
miles are paved and, according to Kaiser, the
remaining 120 miles will be surfaced in 30
mile sections. He estimates the completion
date will be December of 1989. Like most
Tumaquenos, he is optimistic about the
impact of the connecting link. "The road
is the single most important factor for our
development. All else will follow."

Kaiser believes it will be like the trunk
of a tree with branches feeding into it.

The effect will be to open up the entire region. In addition to palm oil, wood, and seafood, the area produces an abundance of coconuts, cacao beans, and fruit. The road will make it possible to bring these to market, and with time, these products could be processed on-site for export. This will require significant investment.

Already government and civic leaders have taken steps to attract capital by declaring the region a "frontier district."

According to Hugo Montano, president of Tumaco's Chamber of Commerce, "One positive step was the signing of Directive 3448 by Colombian President Betancur in 1983. It guarantees that the first 10 years will be tax-free for investors. Another presidential directive reduces the fees required to use the port facilities by 40 percent."

Tumaco has adequate port facilities, but they are virtually deserted. Mayor Kaiser pointed out the problem. "The harbor draft is only about 20 feet. It needs to be dredged out, but until we develop to the point where it is needed for import-export, it is not worth the cost. Our value at this moment is the export of oil. There is a pipeline from the oil-rich areas of Putamayo to Tumaco, [and there] it is pumped aboard tankers for transit to Cartagena. The depth at the station is about 100 feet, so we can handle 150,000-ton ships."

According to Kaiser, 20,000 barrels are pumped daily to large storage tanks to await loading into tankers. He says the completion of another pipeline from the inland city of Neiva to Putumayo will increase this to 70,000 barrels, making Tumaco the main port for the oil-rich areas.

Looking to the future, he pointed out other possibilities. "In 10 to 20 years we could have a road from Tumaco to Putumayo. This would open up not only Colombia's Amazon region, but Brazil's as well, giving them access to the Pacific."

Another facet of Tumaco's development is the need to build a tourist industry. It currently doesn't have the infrastructure to handle significant numbers of tourists. Maria Ortiz, director of the Chamber of Commerce, hopes with time this will change. "In the past the main emphasis has been on developing the Atlantic coast for tourism," she said. "We want to begin to attract tourists by building our first large hotel here capable of accommodating 100 people. This will be done with funds from Nariño investors."

Ortiz knows the task of attracting a tourist trade won't be easy, but she noted, "We have considerable unspoiled areas that are ready for development. El Morro Island, for instance can be reached by bridge in a matter of minutes. It offers nature at its best."

Although not as well publicized, the 1979 earthquake, which heavily damaged the Andean city of Popayan in Nariño, also wreaked havoc on Tumaco, flattening palm trees and destroying many structures. It delayed many projects, but this fertile coastal area is again on the move.

Since the time I chronicle here, some progress has been made, but the area remains largely poor and relatively isolated and undeveloped. Slowly, though, it is inching forward towards a better future. Ecological factors, such as the destruction of mangrove forests and food safety issues have hampered its shrimp production. Although Asia still dominates the farmed shrimp market, by 2004 Colombia was in the world's top 10 producers. They are 5th in the world for palm oil production. In addition, a few luxury hotels have been built, especially in places like El Morro beach. The only thing certain that can still be found in abundance is both the tremendous potential of its natural resources and optimism on the part of its people.

6

A WATER TOWER VIEW OF THE POPE

Everybody loved Pope John Paul II. It didn't matter if you were a politician or the average person, he was held in very high esteem. I found it interesting that even Colombian Marxists guerrillas seemed to love him, seeing him as a revolutionary like them.

Not surprisingly, there was a lot of excitement in all quarters when the Vatican announced that the Pope would visit Colombia. As a prelude to the anticipated visit, I filed some stories like the one below to try and capture the challenging environment that would be the backdrop for his visit.

A Troubled Democracy[6]

Colombia's future is clouded. Its economy is sluggish; its politics unpredictable.

---

6 Adapted from various periodicals, including A Papal visit to a troubled democracy, by Michael Kastre, which appeared in Our Sunday Visitor, June 29, 1986.

And, with 45 percent of the population under 14 years of age, there is tremendous pressure for change. (Only 5 percent of the people are over age 59.)

In a country where there is little or no separation of church and state, one of the strongest unifying factors is the church. Over 95 percent of the population is Catholic. But, as Father Fabio Arturo (a well-known priest in Nariño at the time this story was written)said, "We face a crisis of faith. People are not practicing the teachings of the Church. They come to mass on Sundays, but don't carry the message into their everyday lives."

(In one of my interviews with him, I suggested that this crisis of faith may be caused by the church's failure to help address many of the problems people face. He didn't disagree with me.)

An energetic man, Father Fabio rarely sits still. In an open, candid manner, he noted, "Our problems are deep. There is an immorality, not just sex, but in general. And, of course, there is the violence that plagues us. It's hard to place the blame, but we of the pulpit must question if we are truly putting forth the word of God in such a way that it is heard."

Bishop Arturo Salazar, head of the Diocese of Pasto, agreed that Colombia's problems are linked to a true lack of faith. He specifically noted, "We are in disorder which is caused by injustice. Indeed, injustice has become an institution. The result is violence."

When I asked about the biggest challenge facing the church in Colombia, Salazar responded, "We in the bishops' conference are concerned about a triple idolatry. That is, the worship of money, power, and pleasure. This is related to the injustice I spoke of earlier. Consider the businessman who exploits his employees. Jobs are scarce. People need the work and are in no position to protest. The world cries out for human rights. No doubt human rights have been stepped on. The two are inseparable."

Many of the country's social problems are related to an economy which is a blend of agriculture and manufacturing. In increasing numbers people are flocking to the industrializing urban centers in search of work and a better life. The lack of jobs creates slums and poor health conditions. This in turn puts tremendous strain on the family structure, which, according to Salazar "...is breaking down at an alarming rate."

There is no doubt that Colombians want answers to their problems. Since there is no separation of the Catholic Church and State, as North Americans know it, Colombians see the church as a part of not only the solution, but the problem as well.

Colombian Catholic leaders said that the Pope's visit will heighten awareness and focus the need to reaffirm a living faith and to carry that dedication into the workplace and everyday life. Moreover, they insisted that the Pope's message would not be political, but evangelical.

(I found that statement somewhat confusing, disingenuous, and troubling because without the involvement of politicians and government, meaningful solutions to many issues will be impossible to develop and implement. Voicing my concern about this was one of the factors that almost got me bounced unceremoniously out of a gathering with the Pontiff and a group of fellow journalists and dignitaries.)

Unfortunately, other groups are seeking answers through force. The government's inability to deal effectively with social and economic needs has provided fresh ammunition for the country's powerful guerrilla groups. In addition to combating rebels, the government has to fight a war against a well-entrenched drug mafia.

Despite these problems, the political system is dynamic. It has the mechanisms needed for a peaceful change. Its Congress is split into a House of Representatives and Senate, much like the US system.

Without exception, though, church and public officials see education as the key to a better future. As with other aspects of Colombia, the role of the Catholic Church is critical. Ironically, 75 percent of the country's schools are run by the Church[7].

Father Armando Aguilar, rector for the Jesuit schools in Pasto, explained why he feels the system is failing. "I believe the biggest problem facing Colombia is unemployment. Economic conditions have a strong influence on the schools. Many families, in an effort to survive economically, need to have all members working. This includes the children."

He produced a chart and pointed to some startling statistics from the country's education profile. After going over the

---

7   Although subsequent changes to the Colombian constitution since I wrote this story have tended to separate church and state in terms of education, the Catholic Church still has considerable influence on how and what is taught in public schools. Canon and civil law in Colombia have traditionally been intertwined, making true separation of church and state difficult.

numbers, he illustrated his point by stating that if you started with a base of 1,000 children, there would be 560 with a grammar-school education, but by high school there would only be 160 left. Of these, 20 would eventually reach the university.

Father Aguilar admitted, "It's true that the Church plays a major role in education, but the minister of education sets the policies. If children are allowed to work and not made to attend schools, then the situation will not improve. We simply must provide more teachers and schools and make sure the kids use them."

Bishop Salazar added, "But we have to overcome the custom to fault the current government for all of our problems. Every Colombian has to be a promoter of peace, justice, and love."

Undoubtedly, the pope's journey will improve the chances that, in the future, this becomes reality.

Although long anticipated, in May 1986 we received official Vatican confirmation that the pope would visit Colombia. Two places he was scheduled to visit, Popayan and Tumaco, were in the southwestern region close to where I lived. The government set up a press office to enable journalists to gain the access needed to cover the events. I used my press credentials for Our Sunday Visitor and as a stringer for a small news syndicate in Chicago to obtain a press pass to events in both cities.

In Tumaco, the government had converted an old wooden water tower for the press. It overlooked the square where the Pontiff was scheduled to deliver his address to the people. They had cut windows into it to facilitate taking photos of the event.

I stayed there for a while and had a bird's eye view as the Pope entered the square. But, it turned out to be hotter than hell inside the large tank and I ended up leaving the tower for the cooler streets.

The following is excerpted from one of the stories I filed at the time describing his visit.

The Pilgrim of Hope[8]

He crisscrossed the country, at times going in a single day from cities over a mile-and-a-half high to steamy coastal lowlands and back again. The people he spoke with, like the land, also presented startling contrasts. Compressed into a short time span, his speeches were to youths, powerful politicians, Indians, farmers, jail inmates, religious leaders, street kids, industrialists, union workers, and the aged.

---

8 Excerpted from Pope John Paul: Colombians should strive for peace, by Michael Kastre, which appeared in Our Sunday Visitor, July 20, 1986.

It started on July 1 when a jet carrying Pope John Paul II touched down at Bogota's El Dorado Airport, where he declared, "I am the pilgrim of hope. My heart is open to everyone." Almost a million enthusiastic Colombians lined the streets to greet him. That marked the start of an arduous six-day visit. In all of the 10 cities where he appeared, his theme was direct, his message powerful: all Colombians should strive for peace and an end to the violence that plagues the country.

The trip focused world attention on Colombia, giving Colombians a chance to show that they care about peace and are concerned about order. For John Paul II, the visit was just as crucial.

By the year 2000, one of every two Catholics will be Latin American. Colombia is a cornerstone of democracy and the gateway to South America. In coming here, the Pope emphasized this importance.

Yet, there are problems. In the 1930s, the Catholic Church was viewed as the most stable and unchangeable institution in Latin America. But by the 1960s it had produced some of Colombia's most dedicated revolutionaries. It was the first region in the world to have "guerrilla priests." The first was Father Camilo Torres of Colombia.

Born into an aristocratic family, he was a student in 1948, the same year that Colombia's period of violence began. Fidel Castro, also a student, was on extended travel in Colombia that year. At the time, neither Torres nor Castro became involved, but like the future Cuban leader, Torres never forgot the bloody outbreak. Influenced by the repression and violence, he later joined leftist rebels. Torres was the first man to become a revolutionary symbol by waving a cross instead of a red flag. He opposed violence for change, although in the end he did take up arms. This pattern has since been repeated in Cuba and Nicaragua.

Torres, the first priest with a gun, was a member of a wealthy Bogota family. He joined the ELN in late 1965 after his attempts to create a mass movement for social and political reforms failed, although it did win him a large following as well as many detractors. His efforts, however, helped unite Christians and Marxists for the first time in Colombia.

He died while participating in his first ambush of an army unit in the department of Santander. Inspired by the so-called "Theology of Liberation," other Catholic clergy also became rebels, including Manuel Perez, Jose Jimenez, and Domingo Lain. All came to Colombia because of Torres.

This history is not lost on Pope John Paul II. In a meeting with 2,800 priests and seminarians in Bogota's main cathedral, he asked them to be loyal to the ministry.

The Pope's brief time in Colombia sowed the seeds for some reconciliation between the government and the guerrillas. In Bogota he urged an audience of youths to carefully weigh the moral consequences of taking up arms to force change. In Simon Bolivar Park, he turned his attention to those already fighting. His voice choked with emotion as he said: "I want to ask the guerrillas to use their energies in the spirit of ideals for justice with constructive actions. End the death and destruction of innocent people and indeed, all people." He declared, "The long and cruel years of violence that have affected Colombia have not destroyed the desire to achieve a just peace."

He also asked government leaders to work harder for social reforms to bring peace. In separate meetings, he talked privately to both outgoing President Belisario Betancur and President-elect Virgilio Barco. The actual course Barco takes during the next four years remains to be seen, but most Colombians believe it will be the beginning of a new era of economic prosperity and stability.

Although the crowds displayed emotion and excitement over the presence of the Pope, security remained tight. In the Pacific Coast city of Tumaco, however, the Pope rode in an open truck for the first time since the attempt on his life in 1981. It was here that he also broke another protocol.

Over 30,000 people lined the dusty streets to get a glimpse of the Holy Father. Fifty-year old fisherman Virgilio Arroyo said, "I was trying to see the Pope from my window, but the crowds made this impossible. Then the crowds parted and there he was. I almost collapsed."

Barefoot and dressed in his work clothes, he continued: "I never dreamed the Pope would come into my house. Upon entering, the Pope asked, 'Who is the head of this family?'"

Arroyo replied, "I am." The Pope warmly embraced him and gave his blessing.

In the city of Popayan, the Pope showed his presence was being felt by overruling

his inner circle. It happened when Camilo
Chocue of the Paeces Indian tribe stepped
to the microphone and began reading a
speech. The moment he started talking
about the assassination of Indian priests
Alvaro Ulcue and Pedro Rodrigues, he was
stopped by Father Caicedo. The large
number of Indians in the audience began to
protest. When the Pope realized what was
happening, I saw how visibly upset he was
by the interruption. His words were soft,
but their impact heavy, as he announced
that the speech would continue. After the
ceremonies I watched as he warmly embraced
Chocue, promising to take the text of the
speech to the Vatican and personally study
its contents.

Later Chocue said, "We are always caught
between two fires. First, it was the period
of violence between political parties. Now
we are caught between the military and the
guerrillas. We pray and believe that the
Pope's visit will help to end this."

Publicly, in his 27 speeches, the Pope
had praise for what progress has been made
to correct social problems. Privately, his
dialogue was more direct. A bishop, who
asked not to be named, said, "His visit
will make a difference. Other countries

and the Holy Father himself are seeing that we have good things here. Problems, yes, but also potential and good people. This is a beautiful country. The visit is a stimulus for more progress. He pressed us hard to work more vigorously for reforms and justice. While we are sympathetic to the objectives of the guerrillas, we disagree with their methods."

I asked if "we" meant the Catholic Church. When he hesitated, I asked if he was speaking for the Pope. He simply shrugged and said that no one spoke for the Pope, but the Pontiff himself.

One thing that was clear. That is, wherever he went he left a feeling of optimism and hope in his wake.

I had seen him many times, but the first time I was actually introduced to the Pontiff was in Tumaco. Although I didn't work for Our Sunday Visitor, I was basically a stringer for them in South America. During that brief encounter I was flattered to learn that he had seen many of my OSV stories and was familiar with my name.

Also in Tumaco, as result of my connection with the Catholic press, I was invited to a coffee klatch of sorts. There were probably 30 people in the room seated around a large dark rectangular wooden table, with the Pope positioned at the end of it. The walls were beige colored stucco accented by rich oil paintings of Colombian coastal scenes and pueblos. A large rustic wooden cross hung on the wall closest to John Paul. (I didn't know if it had been scripted by some clever Church official, but if it was, they had succeeded in creating the right effect.) Flecks of dust drifted through the air in the sunlight that streamed through a window on the side of the space. It seemed the perfect setting for the Pontiff to hold court.

The majority of people in the room appeared to be journalists, with a handful of scarlet clad cardinals, bishops, local politicians, and security personnel scattered around. I didn't really know what the rules were. It certainly wasn't a question and answer type

Pope John Paul II riding through the streets of Tumaco.

press conference. Nonetheless, a venerable reporter from one the country's large daily newspapers raised his hand and lobbed the Pontiff a soft ball question. Basically he asked the Pope how he assessed the trip in terms of pushing forward some type of peace between the rebels and government.

The Pope gave the obligatory response that he was optimistic, but much work remained to be done. At that point I decided to weigh in. Instead of raising my hand, I stood and in English asked, "Holy Father, I know you have strongly indicated that your journey is evangelical and not political, but how can you impact the peace process without also getting involved in the politics and socioeconomic issues that are at the root of the crisis facing the country and all Colombians?"

The room grew very quiet as heads turned in my direction. I added, "I have heard you talk about the social reforms needed and urging people to live better Christian lives. That is certainly important, but again it would seem as though the government needs to take the lead and legislate such reforms."

I saw a flash of red out of the corner of my eye as an older cardinal slid up next to me and whispered in my ear, telling me my questions were inappropriate. I merely listened as he then suggested perhaps I should leave the gathering. My face flushed from embarrassment. Without waiting for a reply the cardinal motioned to a uniformed policeman standing against the wall and the cop moved in towards me.

The room started to buzz, eyes looking in my direction and then back at the Pope. Then, after a slight feeble wave from the Pontiff, the Cardinal took a step back and clasped his hands in front of his cassock. The policeman stopped in his tracks.

Everyone, including me, looked at the Pope. His head was characteristically bowed. He trembled slightly and appeared frail, as he had ever since the attempt on his life in 1981 in St. Peter's Square in Vatican City. He peered at me with alert eyes and what I perceived at the time to be a gaze that instantly evaluated me with perhaps a hint of humor or amusement.

He spoke softly and slowly, but forcefully in heavily accented English. "I understand the provocative nature of your question, but I am not a politician. My concern is for not only my flock, but all peoples. I don't presume to tell others how to run their affairs. What I do is express the doctrines of universal love and tolerance and urge social justice."

That's all I got. His eyes searched the room and he nodded at another journalist. Thereafter, when he would see me during his visit, he would give me a slight bow and a subtle, enigmatic smile of sorts. The man definitely was not shy about using his power to intervene with those who sought to insulate him from the public.

While he received wide-spread support from most quarters during his visit, there were some very vocal critics at the time who were skeptical that mere words by the Pontiff would make a difference. Today those same critics point out that Colombia has changed in terms of stability and made some progress as a result of a strong-willed president—one who was willing to militarily go after the rebels. Despite this, they are quick to say that progress has come at a cost of trampling on the civil rights of some groups.

From my perspective, I saw the changes first hand and believe the striking before and after statistics speak for themselves. As for the right balance, I'll leave that subjective debate to others.

One thing rang particularly true during the Pope's trip as he tried to heal some of the country's deepest wounds. He summed it up in Chinchina when he said, "You must look to the past, not just to see the glory, but to find your own roots and adequate answers to the facts of history in order to face and reach moral and religious preparation for the future."

Few would argue with that. I certainly didn't at the time, nor do I now.

After traipsing around Tumaco in the wake of the Pope, I procured a taxi boat and retreated to my tiny rented cabana on Boca Grande beach. The no frills hotel consisted of a series of rustic shacks on the isolated beach. I loved this desolate perpetually windswept stretch of the Pacific Ocean. I sat in front of my temporary one room abode and balanced my typewriter on my lap and wrote the story that the account above was excerpted from.

Early the next the morning I took a boat back to town, went to the telecom office, paid for a connection to the US, and read my story to Lou Jacquet, my OSV editor at the time, as it was copied down.

Ah, if I had had the Internet at that time life would have been so much simpler. Or maybe it wouldn't have been because you had to get up close and personal to someone like the Pope to get a story and not merely Google the background and color.

7

CONVERSATIONS WITH A GUERRILLA IN A SALT
CATHEDRAL

I certainly had no wish to be kidnapped, but one of
the things I wanted to do was interview a guerrilla and
listen to their story and how they thought. Yet, it wasn't
exactly like they were listed in the telephone directory.
Presented with the challenge of how to facilitate such a
meeting, I pursued all avenues that seemed promising.

Fortunately, in the autumn of 1986, Armando
introduced me to a woman who ran a bar in Tumaco.
One of the things she claimed was that she was the
cousin of the notorious guerrilla, Pizarro. As with many
rebels, though, myth, legend, and rumor surrounded
the man, which only gave me a murky sense of him and
a determination to separate fact from fiction.

With no Internet, my resources for research were
limited. Undeterred, I started at the archives of the
local paper. I reasoned that at the very least I could get

a photograph of the man, which I did. Next I tried to corroborate news accounts with the few contacts I had with the police. Finally, I visited DAS (the equivalent of our FBI) in an effort to gain more information. I was not as well connected to DAS as I was with police officials and my inquiries were met with what I can only describe as hostile suspicion. Nonetheless, what emerged from all this was that Pizarro was an interesting character, to say the least.

The son of a navy admiral, Carlos Pizarro enlisted in the guerrilla group the Revolutionary Armed Forces of Colombia, also known as FARC. Its operations were primarily focused on military action in rural areas. Pizarro disagreed with the group's commanders and wanted to take the fight to the cities. As a result, he left the FARC in the early 1970s and helped establish the M-19 guerrilla group.

Arrested in the late 1970s, he spent three years in La Picota jail in Bogota before being released. Following the siege on the Palace of Justice and the killing of top M-19 leadership, he became the movement's military commander. Known for his aggressiveness, he tried unsuccessfully to establish a group called the "America Battalion," comprised of Colombian rebels and foreign fighters from other Latin American countries as well.

Pizarro was certainly progressive and innovative. By the late 1980s, he had begun negotiations with the Colombian government for demobilization of the M-19 based on certain conditions, primarily a full pardon for all prior activities and the right to form a political party.

Following the signing of an accord with the government he announced he would run as the group's presidential candidate in the 1990 national elections. But the 39 year old rebel was assassinated aboard a plane in April of 1990 by a young paramilitary (right wing) rebel named Gerardo Gutierrez Uribe. He was not alone in his demise. Luis Carlos Galan, the leading liberal presidential candidate and Bernardo Jaramillo Ossa, the presidential candidate for the Union Patriotica—another guerrilla-based political party—were also assassinated in the same election.

At the time I lived in Colombia, though, when I inquired of his supposed cousin in Tumaco if she thought it might be possible to set up an interview with him she said she would try. But nothing was promised or definite.

Curious about the shift from guns to politics to achieve the reform they sought, I wanted to hear Pizarro's thinking and strategy. I understood how operating in the countryside was radically different than trying to ferment a revolution in urban areas. Recruiting country folks, including kids often as young as 13 or 14 years of age, and holding large tracks of sparsely populated rural areas was one thing. Hiding and waging warfare in an urban jungle was something else entirely.

Colombia has one of the highest urbanization rates of any Latin American nation, with over 75 percent of the population living in cities. To be sure, there are plenty of poor people to stir up and recruit from in the cities, but it's also obviously where the most powerful presence of police and military is concentrated. Such an approach would be a radical departure from models such as Castro's Cuban revolution where he swept down from the mountains to gain control of the countryside before he attacked the center of power in Havana. The ongoing Colombian revolution was also changing from its original underpinning in other, often unexpected ways. I wanted to explore and document that evolution.

The Roots of Revolution

Since it's not a recent trend, understanding the rise and framing the mentality of armed rebels in Colombia requires a look at the climate and events that spawned the guerrilla movements. It goes back to the Cold War and the ideological struggle between communism and capitalism. The 1940s and 50s Colombia, with its colonial legacy of inequitable wealth distribution, had the perfect conditions for the rise of Marxist movements. Things were so volatile that the period from 1948 to 1966 is known as La Violencia or the Period of Violence. During that time over 200,000 people were killed.

A single act proved to be the flashpoint that ignited the violence. Specifically, in the late 1940s dissident Jorge Eliecer Gaitan had emerged from the liberal and communist led agrarian and labor reform movements to become a leading presidential candidate. In April of

1948, though, he was gunned down on a street in Bogota. This assassination triggered massive demonstrations and the beginning of clashes between liberals and conservatives that lasted for almost two decades.

My father-in-law used to tell me that during that time you could get shot for the color of tie you wore. (I believe he said the liberals wore red and the conservatives wore blue, but I am not sure.) There was a lull in the bloody battles in the late 1950s and early 60s when moderate leftists and conservatives started to work out a compromise, but the worldwide surge in leftist activism in the 1960s reignited the violence.

To be sure, it was much more complex than the snapshot provided here. For example, the Liberal Party abstained from the 1950 presidential election, which was won uncontested by conservative Laureano Gomez. The Gomez administration was supported by the Catholic Church, which had been victimized during the Period of Violence. It was also supported by the US, which viewed Communist Party support for peasants as a Cold War threat in what it considered its own backyard.

Despite this murky mix of support, Gomez was overthrown by a military coup that saw General Gustavo Rojas Pinilla come to power. (It was one of the few times in the country's history that the military stepped in to seize control.)

Despite the strongman's actions, more clashes and struggles followed. By the late 1960s and early 1970s, though, cooler heads had started to prevail and a power sharing agreement worked out that saw the two main parties begin to alternate presidential terms. Things continued to return to normal politics from there.

But the seeds for the birth of the leftist guerrilla groups had been planted during La Violencia. Despite the calm that had been restored to Colombian politics, the rebels got a boost starting in the 1970s and continuing into the 1980s by cashing in as they provided muscle for the cocaine cartels in exchange for funding. Moreover, just as left wing movements like the FARC and ELN (Ejercito de Liberacion Nacional) evolved, other forces also came into existence as right wing militias emerged as a force for the "haves."

This created an environment where you not only had Marxists rebels, but armed conservative right wing groups, too. Known as paramilitares or autodefensas they were formed by the landholders and wealthy and transformed into standing armies. In the past, Colombia's military even tended to turn a blind eye toward these groups since they often shared similar objectives, which was to defeat the leftists. They also received significant money and weapons from the US. Under leaders like Carlos Castano Gil, the United Self Defense Forces of Colombia (Autodefensas Unidas de Colombia or AUC) was created as an umbrella organization of regional far-right groups. At one point it is estimated that they had over 20,000 fighters in uniform.

The AUC committed horrendous massacres of civilians, who were allegedly guerrilla sympathizers, and terrorized the countryside as much as the opposition leftists. One of the AUC's techniques was to simply kill off young people in villages who supported the FARC or ELN, thereby eliminating potential future combatants. Like the Marxists, they were also financed in large measure with drug money. They were finally designated as a terrorist organization by the US and the European Union. Today, they have largely been disbanded and their leaders prosecuted.

All of this turmoil set the stage for the perfect storm that was 1980s Colombia as everything changed even more.

The Death of an Ideology

The 1980s marked dramatic shifts in the guerrilla movements in Colombia as myriad factors all converged. Marxist ideology was starting to take a backseat to practicalities. The fall of the Soviet Union dried up money to satellite communist countries like Cuba. In turn, they could no longer fund Colombia's guerrilla groups. Without money to operate, the rebels started looking for alternative resources to wage their Marxist war. Moreover, the rebels' fledging political initiatives lacked the funding they required to seriously challenge the status quo at the ballot box.

At the time, Colombia's powerful cocaine cartels were under increasing pressure from the government.

The mafia had the financial resources, but not the manpower to fully protect their interests. This made the cartels and the guerrilla movements natural allies in many respects.

Although powerful, it wasn't a perfect alliance by any means. The guerrillas began to not just provide protection, but in some cases they tried to muscle in on illegal drug activities. They also embarked on a campaign to kidnap everyone from rich and prominent businessmen to politicians and journalists in their bid to gain money and try to win the public relations war by intimidating news outlets and terrorizing Colombian civilians.

In effect, their long standing strategy and ideology related to social justice, equal opportunity, and political and economic reform were lost as their communist ideals were exchanged for outright criminal and terrorist activities.

This was the backdrop for which I sought to sit down and talk to a guerrilla leader. I was excited when Armando called with a message that Pizarro had agreed to meet me in Tumaco. I was nervous with anticipation and went two days early to ensure that all the details of the meeting were in place. I wanted to meet him in a public place, but was told that someone would pick me up at the hotel and drive me to a rendezvous location close by. I was a little uncomfortable with this arrangement, but reluctantly agreed when I was told that was the only way. My one condition was that I insisted Armando accompany me to translate. Finally it was set.

Since the pick-up was scheduled for dusk, we ate an early dinner and camped out in the small lobby of our hotel. Darkness came and we waited, pacing and smoking. Finally after 9 pm Pizarro's cousin sent word, asking us to join her in the bar.

We still didn't know what had happened, but she enlightened us by saying Pizarro was unable to meet with us that day and wasn't sure when he would be available.

I was disappointed and upset, but occasional disappointment was part of doing business. I returned home to Pasto and put the matter on the back burner in my mind, convinced there would be other opportunities. Several weeks passed. My wife went to Bogota to visit her parents and my mornings were spent getting the girls off to school. On one such morning I had just settled into my office after getting the kids on the Montessori van when our housekeeper told me I had a visitor.

An old dented white Renault was parked at the curb in front of the house. My visitor was an average looking man I guessed to be in his late 20s. At first I thought he was making a delivery of some sort or someone looking for money or work. I felt my heart thump when he simply asked me to go with him to meet someone.

"Pizarro?" I inquired.

All I got to that question was a slight smile and a

shake of his head.

"Alright," I agreed, "but I have to get my translator."

Again a shake of his head and he added, "Solamente tu." (Only you.)

Without having time to process the situation, I grabbed my camera bag and multi-pocketed vest with my steno pad, smokes, and a recorder off the foyer coat rack and climbed into his car.

It would turn out not to be an interview, but rather a conversation in a bar in a seedy part of town by the bus station. From there it transitioned into a debate at some point.

My heart was beating so wildly I wondered if I might actually be having a heart attack as I was escorted into a long rectangular room. A scarred wooden bar with a brick base ran the length of one wall. The remainder of the space was filled with square tables flanked on all four sides by mismatched chairs. The obvious leader sat in the corner and several very alert men were scattered around the room all staring at me. A couple of them had what appeared to be machine pistols prominently displayed on their tables.

The first thing that struck me was that I had studied photos of Pizarro and this guy wasn't him. He had the same mustache and scraggily beard that many revolutionaries favored, but it wasn't the right face. At first I was momentarily confused, but before I could say anything he kicked a chair out from under his table and made a sweeping gesture for me to sit.

The first words out of his mouth were, "Where are you from?"

Without thinking I replied, "I was born in Michigan, but raised in Arizona."

"The cold and the hot," he said.

"Your English is very good," I blurted out.

"What did you expect, some uneducated campesino? (Loosely translated means hick or red neck.)

I sat. "To be honest, I wasn't sure what to expect."

I was shaking a little, but pulled out my pocket tape recorder and a pack of Marlboros from my vest and casually set them on the table.

He immediately snatched up the recorder and removed the tape from it and slid both of them back to me. "No tape, no pictures."

"I thought the purpose of talking was for me to write a story about you and your cause."

"First we talk off the record. I like to know who I am dealing with. Some reporters would twist my words and make me look bad."

I pulled out a steno pad and started writing, saying, "Mind if I take notes?"

He shrugged noncommittally, appearing to be interested in what I was scribbling. "How can you write so fast?"

"It's my own form of shorthand. Basically I eliminate most of the vowels from words."

"Clever."

"To be honest I was hoping to meet with Pizarro."

"Instead you got me, but we fight for the same cause."

"Okay. Suppose we start with your name."

He studied me for a moment then gave me a name. Although I hadn't asked him yet, he then went on to give me a quick sketch of his background, a sort of verbal resume.

I was unfamiliar with the name at the time, but learned later that he was in fact one of Pizarro's compatriots. I refer to him here, though, only as "Jaime." Although heavily accented, his English was excellent and he explained that he had studied engineering (mechanical I think) at a major east coast university in the US. It also turned out that he had a lot of family in the US, mostly in Jackson Heights in Queens, New York. I recall that one was a medical doctor.

I was a little more relaxed with the niceties out of the way and wanted to get to my questions.

Before I could, though, he abruptly asked, "You married? Kids?"

"Yes."

"I knew that. You have a nice home."

I stopped being relaxed.

He seemed to be reading my mind. "A little respect is healthy or should I say a little fear?"

I must have look scared, confused or both because he laughed. "I just meant I know all about you. You don't exactly live a secret life here."

At that moment the thought that he really did know where I lived hit home. In my haste and excitement to arrive at the meeting, I hadn't focused on that thought before. I suppose in a way that wasn't surprising because at the time there were only eight foreigners in the entire department, but I was the only gringo. So it wasn't like I was really blending in with my new environment.

My mind went into overdrive. Nagging at my thoughts was the doctor friend Nydia and I had. He and his wife and kids lived a block from us in our neighborhood. He told us how periodically men would come in the night and basically kidnap him to provide medical attention to injured rebels. Admittedly, though, they always returned him home unharmed within a few days. I recall him telling us his chilling account of the first time. He said he awoke in the night to find two armed men standing in his bedroom. They proceeded to direct him to get dressed and accompany them. That night after hearing the story my wife begged me not take foolish chances, but here I was in a room full of armed men talking politics and socials issues with committed rebels.

I awkwardly doodled on my pad and avoided his eyes as we sat in silence for what seemed like several long minutes, but was probably only a few seconds. He lightened the mood by signaling for one of his men to bring something to drink. The man brought two shot glasses, a large bottle of aquardiente, and a small bottle of Bretana, which is Colombian club soda.

He filled the glasses and we silently raised them and, in the Colombian tradition, knocked them back in a single gulp. My throat burned.

"Okay, to business. First, since you gringos love labels so much, let me ask about your politics before you ask me about mine."

I decided to be direct. "I love freedom and I'm an avowed capitalist. I do, however, understand the desire and need for reform where inequities exist."

"Fair enough and spoken like a true diplomat. I'm a communist. Too few people control too much of the dollars."

"Okay. Who would you say are the leaders you admire most?"

"Castro. And Mao did a lot for his people."

I wanted to avoid appearing critical and cynical. At the same time I wanted to challenge him on what had always been a confusing mystery to me so I tried to choose my words carefully. "I've never understood the fascination with Castro, although I will admit that he did what he said he would do."

"What's that?"

"He certainly made everyone the same—poor. And, I think he is a hypocrite because he has elections, but is the only candidate, effectively, in his own words, making himself 'president for life.'"

"It's more complex than that. He had to redistribute the wealth before building a new system."

"It's been over 25 years..."

He looked angry for the first time. "You gringos run around the world and seem to believe that everyone wants democracy. I assure you they don't. Besides, all that means is that people vote."

I saw the mixture of anger and frustration on his face. (Even today his words make me a bit uneasy with the US role in world politics.)

"Don't you find it arrogant that you think because that is your view, that everyone should just accept it? Our poor are not like your poor."

I felt like I was back in college in the radical 1960s debating social and political issues with my more liberal friends, but pressed him. "How are they different?" I asked. "Poor is poor."

"Your poor are not poor. Many are overfed and fat. They have cars, TVs. The government pays them."

"Then I rest my case," I responded. "Democracy works."

He ignored my comment and smiled at me like he was a professor and I was the slow student in the class. "We love gringos, but are not so sure about your country."

I couldn't resist and said, "Then why are people standing in line for visas or sneaking into America to live there? I don't see them doing that to get into Cuba or China."

Again, the flash of anger and he continued as if I hadn't spoken. "You even have the ignorance and arrogance to call yourselves Americans. Living in the Americas, we are all Americans. You are North Americans and we are South Americans. So, being American is not unique to you. You are not special."

I stopped taking notes and trying to write a transcript of the conversation as it unfolded. I wanted to fully engage him, look him in the eye, and not merely scribble notes and glance at him. Our spirited exchange lasted another hour. He kept spouting what I considered to be Marxist clichés and I kept trying to hammer home my points. Ironically, looking back, I probably evoked as many clichés as he did, but at the moment I felt like I was scoring.

At some point during our debate he started to grudgingly admit that things were not as pure as he would have me believe. We never got very far into how they were becoming like the mafia with kidnappings and illegal drugs, but he did say that was a legitimate strategy to battle an illegitimate government.

I countered with how he apparently thought it was right to recruit young teenagers who couldn't possibly have the experience or maturity to understand what they were fighting for. He admitted that it wasn't a perfect world and revolution always had innocent casualties as he called them.

I pressed the point that they should use the ballot box instead of bullets. He shot back that this was one of the strategies they had begun to pursue, but he complained that the media was a propaganda machine controlled by the establishment. The result was that the public relations war was being manipulated and the people voting were misinformed. If they knew the truth or really thought about conditions they would overwhelmingly support change.

When one of his men approached him and whispered in his ear it was abruptly over.

We shook hands; and, as he regarded me, he shook his head. "You should help us. We will talk again."

I wasn't sure what his suggestion meant. Perhaps he wanted me to write stories favorable to his cause. For the moment, though, that was it. He turned and disappeared through the back door, his men glancing at me as they filed out after him.

I left by the front door and walked down the street into another bar and tried to make sure my notes made sense. I also tried to fill in some of the conversation that had occurred after I stopped taking notes.

It would be over a month before I was contacted again. This time a voice on the phone simply told me to be in the main chapel of the salt cathedral on a certain day at a specific time. I knew who it was immediately and without hesitation I packed and drove to Bogota early in the afternoon. I arrived the following day— almost two days early.

After arriving in Bogota and spending the night at my in-laws I went to the church the day before the meeting. At the time I thought it was an odd place to meet with a rebel, but I shrugged it off and studied the magnificent place. It was unlike any other religious site I had ever visited and I knew I had to capture it even before the meeting. The following is summarized from one of the stories I filed at the time.

An Underground Church in a Mountain of Salt[9]
===

One of the truly great houses of the Lord does not have stained-glass windows or spires reaching toward the heavens. It is high in the Andes, but is not warmed by the sun because it lies within a mountain. The creation of an underground cathedral, carved out of salt, took a couple centuries and was an act of faith and sacrifice perhaps unparalleled in the Americas.

The mountain of salt was originally the treasure of the Muiscas Indians in what is now Colombia. They processed the salt into sparkling white blocks for commercial use, primarily for preserving food. The arrival of explorers in South America dramatically changed life for the natives.

Lured by the golden legend of El Dorado, the Spanish landed in Colombia late in the 15th century. Eventually, General Jimenez de Quesada pushed inland from the Atlantic coast. His expedition fought indigenous tribes, unknown illnesses, and vegetation that threatened to engulf them within its tentacles. As they struggled to reach the interior, Spanish scouts returned with salt

---

9　Excerpted from An Underground Church in a Mountain of Salt, by Michael Kastre, which appeared in Our Sunday Visitor, December 14, 1986.

loaves found on the banks of the Magdelena River. Because the salt was not extracted from sea water, the general was anxious to find the source.

He climbed the high valleys of the Andes, conquered the Muiscas and named the region Nuevo Reino de Granada. Quesada discovered the salt source in the Indian pueblo of Zipaquira, and 25 miles away he founded Santa Fe De Bogota, what would become the Colombian capital.

The Spaniards continued to process the salt that oozed from the cracks in the mountain. Later, to increase production, they began to dig crude tunnels into the mountain and the mine was born. Progress was slow, however, and the lack of sound mining techniques hindered excavation for many years.

According to Colombian historian Don Luis Orjuela, German engineer Jacob Wiesner started to excavate the main tunnel in 1808. For the miners it was a dangerous existence. Daily they risked their lives with inadequate tools, cave-ins, lethal gases, and over a century of darkness pierced only by tallow candles.

With life hanging on a thin thread and their health escaping with each breath, the miners of Zipaquira raised their eyes to heaven, even though they could scarcely see more than a few feet in the darkness that engulfed them.

As the tunnels and openings were progressing, a rough little altar also progressed. On it was placed a simple painting of the Virgin Mary. Candles burned in front of the painting, making it a beacon of hope to the miners. The devotion of the miners led to their desire to erect a more permanent monument to St. Mary in the form of a statue.

The mine had become a shrine from what had been an industrial endeavor. Yet, the final consecration of the great salt mine was not complete. To transform the tunnels and caverns created by the miners required yet another artist. The Bank of the Republic, which administered the mines, chose architect Jose Gonzalez Concha to build a church. He foresaw the cathedral in the shapeless tunnels and galleries. He envisioned expanding the openings and supporting them with massive columns, using indirect lighting to preserve the natural beauty of the interior.

Concha, in his report to bank officials said, "It would have been a great mistake

to transform the interior of the mines
into the style of any church already in
existence, either old-fashioned or modern.
Common architecture, created for open air
in the interior of a salt mine would become
poor and expressionless, even if it were
constructed with excellent and precious
materials. Instead, I have tried to enhance
the majestic arches sculptured in the salt
rock through the humble efforts of the
miners and consecrate them to the glory
of the faith, transforming the rough and
primitive work into a hymn of praise to the
Creator."

The site of the church was blessed by
Monsignor Antonio Samore, apostolic nuncio
to Pope Pius XII, on October 7, 1950. Work
started the following year. Four years
later, the cathedral was inaugurated and
blessed by Bishop Tulio Botero of the
Diocese of Zipaquia.

Nestled at 8,000 feet in the Andes,
the pueblo of 40,000 has remained largely
unchanged. The mines still have four
levels. The cathedral occupies the second
level, but the others continue to produce
125,000 bags of salt per month. Because it
is buried within the mountain, construction
of the massive cathedral has not changed

Zipaquira's low skyline. Its size and beauty are hidden. With its four aisles, each 400 feet long, it has 60,000 square feet, making it larger than St. Peter's Basilica in Rome. It can accommodate 8,000 people. The ceiling is 200 feet high and is supported by 14 large columns. The base of each is 900 square feet, banded by heavy steel cables to prevent cracking. There are sculptures of angels, saints, and a manger scene. The 18-ton altar is carved from rock salt. The entrance to the Salt Cathedral is a tunnel 1,400 feet long.

Like the men who shaped it over the centuries, the style and beauty of the cathedral are unique.

Steeped in history, sweat, and sacrifice, this then was the setting I walked into to meet with Jaime. With the steady stream of tourists it attracts, perhaps my revolutionary friend felt he could blend in easily. But as I made my way down the long tunnel, I found it odd that a man in his line of work would chose a site with only one entrance. With those thoughts, I settled into the main chamber at the designated spot and waited.

Without turning, I sensed when men settled in on the wooden pew behind me. In the semidarkness I casually reached in my vest pocket and switched on my micro recorder. Jaime then squeezed in next to me, knelt and crossed himself, which I found odd for an avowed Marxist. Our little group was alone in the back of the big cathedral, with few pilgrims visiting the shrine because it was a weekday.

"So what do you really want?" he finally asked.

"A proper interview."

He ignored my response, slid sideways and peered at my face, and asked, "In coming here did you consider betraying me to the authorities?"

"I'm a journalist, not a cop or a spy."

He laughed. "I actually believe you. You are not the type and besides I know how much you love those little girls of yours."

Hearing those words, my face must have betrayed me and he added, in a playful tone, "You need to have a little humor, gringo."

"I came here to talk. Are you going to talk to me?"

"Go ahead."

There had been an escalating series of bombings, kidnappings, and violent ambushes during that time, so I asked, "Why put the country through such violent turmoil?"

"All revolutions start at the point of a gun."

"I don't believe that. How about the ballot box? If the majority of people want change it will happen."

"Do you remember the last time we talked? The establishment controls the propaganda machine. Five percent of the population control 95 percent of the wealth of my country. But people are complacent. They have given up. They need to be inspired to rise up."

"And blowing up things and kidnapping people is going to accomplish that?"

I could sense his frustration with me. "We are taking the fight to the cities, where the people live. It's like a fuse and eventually it will be ignited."

"Many would say you have lost your ideals and have become criminals."

He cursed in Spanish. Crossed himself, then cursed at himself in English. "You do what you have to do to survive."

I decided not to belabor the point and asked, "Apparently not everyone in your group agrees with you."

"About what?"

"Trying to achieve change by other means."

He was not amused and snapped at me. "Be specific."

"Some of your brothers are beginning to form political parties. If that approach is so ineffective, why bother?"

"You are not stupid. You know that there are many ideas within groups."

"I take it your ideas are not in the majority?"

"I wouldn't say that, but I don't make those kinds of decisions."

I was clutching my steno pad in the dim light. At that point he regarded me with a suspicious stare. "Why aren't you writing this down?"

I decided to be honest. "I'm taping it."

He glared at me. "You have cojones (loosely translated this means "balls" in Spanish). I'll give you that. Okay, tape away, but absolutely no photos."

"Do you think you are winning?"

"We have made a lot of progress and the government keeps making concessions."

"Concessions in how they deal with you, but nothing has changed for the ordinary citizen."

"Progress is progress. We are right and we will win in the end."

"Will that end poverty and corruption?"

"When any government is accountable only from the top, corruption becomes a way of life. We will be different."

"Do you really believe that? Look at Cuba."

"Nothing is perfect, but the present system has ensured its own fall."

"Do you think China under Mao was a great success?"

He evaded the question and said, "We are not Chinese."

"Mao preached pride in poverty. The only problem was that at some point nobody believed him anymore. In fact, just like the Russians, the government learned that there is no pride or productivity if people aren't free. I believe the Cubans will eventually learn the same lesson."

"Do you call the inequities that exist in Colombia, where the rich control everything, freedom?"

"I hate to be repetitive, but you still have elections."

The Cathedral's main alter.

"And you call me an idealist. What you say is pure gringo bullshit. Look, to understand you have to stop looking at us and our struggle through the eyes of a gringo."

"It just seems like you are trying to repeat the mistakes of others. I believe history has repeatedly shown that imposing communism, or whatever you call it, regardless of the brand, simply doesn't work no matter how well meaning the theory is."

We seemed to share a moment at that instant and I said, "I feel like I'm back at the university in some dorm room having the same old debate with those who were idealist and liberal."

"We can agree on that. I went to school in your

country and know what you are talking about. Are you here to convert me or to interview me?"

"I'm just trying to understand what your group is all about and what it hopes to achieve."

"You need to talk to others. We have decided that you can have the interview you want, but you will have to visit us in the country."

"Who's we?"

"Let's just leave it at that for now. We'll be in touch."

He stood and said, "After you."

Unsure of what to do, I stood and turned towards the main tunnel. Glancing back I didn't see Jaime or his men so I just kept walking. The air grew warmer as I trudged up the incline. I tried to evaluate how it had gone. I pulled out my recorder and hit rewind and then played some of the tape. It was a bit muffled, but perfectly audible.

At the surface, I sat in my car, wanting to see him leave. My Yashica camera fitted with a telephoto lens lay on the seat next to me. Unconsciously out of habit I removed the lens cover and brought it up and rested it on the steering wheel as he emerged followed closely by two other men.

I peered through the view finder and focused on his face. With the magnification I could see it clearly. For a brief moment he seemed to look directly at me, although I was sure he couldn't see me clearly. There was the trace of a smile. Then he pulled his cap lower and turned away. I suppose I was relieved that I had not pulled the shutter and shot him. To do otherwise would have been a violation of the rules of engagement I had agreed to. Yet, I wondered if he knew I had held up my end of the bargain. The ball was in his court to set another meeting, hopefully with Pizarro himself. I expected to hear from him at some point. I did. It was not, however, the message I had expected. It happened over a month later when he called our home in Pasto.

I recognized his voice right away. He was all business. He said things were changing. I asked what that meant and he simply said he would never harm me or my family, but that he couldn't speak for others in his cause. He mentioned how reporters had become favorite targets for murder and kidnapping in the most recent violence.

The hair literally stood up on the back of my neck at that point. I still recall his words. "Reporters can be used for propaganda or worse and this is not the way I want to find out if you are a macho or just a well-meaning periodista (reporter) seeking truth and understanding. Go home gringo."

Rattling around in my brain at that moment was the thought of the spate of recent murders of reporters across the country. I knew I was no longer just a student of the situation, detached and observing from a distance. Like it or not, this was real and could happen to anyone. I asked if his advice was based on something he specifically had seen or heard. He only answered by repeating that I should go home.

The brief call was beyond unsettling and I vividly remember going out that night with a group of friends and getting thoroughly drunk. Ironically, I sat the entire night with my back to the wall and facing the entrance to the bar as though that would protect me.

In the end, I was left to put into context my experience and ponder the future of not only Colombia, but my own as well. Indeed, my conversations with this rebel leader would become one of the major factors in a decision that would alter the course of my future.

Later, when I was back in the US, I thought of Jaime every time I saw a news item where a reporter was murdered or a newspaper bombed—over 75 reporters have been killed in Colombia since the 1980s, most for reporting on corruption, the mafia, and guerrilla activities. Then, as now, the impact was dramatic. Most notably, the 1986 murder (ordered by Pablo Escobar) of Guillermo Cano, publisher of Colombia's big daily newspaper, El Espectador, which shook the foundations of the country to its very core. Cano had taken a strong stance against drugs and was a staunch supporter of the extradition of Colombian drug traffickers to the US to face trial. It's a land where newspaper publishers carry considerable weight and command respect. In addition, this was at a time when the president of the Supreme Court, the minister of justice, and the director of the national police had all been murdered. And, the head of their equivalent of our FBI had survived seven assassination attempts.

My most recent inquiries (2009) on Jaime's current whereabouts or fate yielded mixed reports. One source said he had been shot on the Colombian-Venezuelan border in a battle with the army. Others said he was alive and out of the movement and involved in politics, which I found interesting, although like me he would be much older today. It may well turn out that I will never know and it will remain a mystery to me or a matter of speculation.

I also find myself thinking about matters other than his fate. Then, as now, I periodically mull over my conversations with Jaime and chide myself for clearly breaking one of the fundamental rules of journalism. My job was to ask questions and get answers. Our meetings should have been about him and his views, not mine. I failed when I started to give him my opinions, biases, and interjecting myself into the interview. I allowed it to turn into a debate filled with clichés. I probably also reinforced his image of gringos as know it alls, thinking our way is the only right way.

Yet, no matter the nature of the talks with this likable rebel leader, it did provide a certain layer of understanding into the age old struggle between the have and have nots in a present day society steeped in many elements of ancient feudalism. Perhaps proving once again that the more things change, the more they stay the same.

8

INTERVIEW AND END OF AN ANTI-DRUG CZAR

It was during the 1980s that the Colombian cocaine cowboys, especially the Medellin Cartel, were at the height of their power. This time was marked by the partnership of the drug lords and rebels. This signaled not only the confluence of criminal activities and Marxists guerrillas, but was a period when those events really started to have a significant impact on the country's courts, economy, and politics as well. No aspect of Colombian life was immune. Colombian democracy was under direct assault. The threat of violence and death impacted the economy, exacerbated inflation, distorted income distribution, skewed real estate values, corrupted the courts and public officials, and swayed local and national elections.

It's important to point out that even though the cocaine trade has had a strong influence on the country, the overwhelming majority of Colombians are honest, hardworking, and charming people who didn't (then or now) have anything to do with illegal drugs. To say otherwise is simply not true. Having married into a large and wonderful Colombian family, I have seen first-hand how unfortunate it is that so many foreigners tend to view the typical Colombian as somehow associated with the unsavory business. Those involved with the cartels are literally a handful of individuals out of forty plus million Colombians.

Given the palpable feeling of a "wild west" environment and atmosphere created within Colombia by the increasingly powerful cocaine cartels, I started contacting the US Embassy in Bogota for related interviews. I believed that people, especially foreigners, needed to understand what was going on and how illegal drugs were dramatically impacting life in faraway places like the US and Europe.

Initially, I focused on trying to talk to US Drug Enforcement Agency (DEA) personnel posted in Colombia. This proved difficult to arrange because those DEA agents understandably feared the very real threat of being killed by the drug mafia if they were identified. They did, however, prove to be extremely professional and obliging. They helped to arrange meetings with officials, including one with Colombia's top drug cop whose identity was publically available.

That particular interview took place in the most unusual set up I have ever witnessed for such a meeting. The following is a look at the times and events leading up to this meeting and the tragic end of an extraordinary man's life.

When Cocaine Masqueraded as Harmless

The real underlying reason things happen is too often completely overlooked or too unlikely to consider. Even when we look back it's hard to fathom that people once believed a certain way. Part of what ignited the spectacular rise of cocaine use in places like the US, for example, was because of prevailing attitudes at the time. This was actually fueled in no small part by the media, many of whom wrote stories that tended to underestimate the dangers and even glamorize the lure of cocaine.

Specifically, there was a time in the 1980s when, just like the days of alcohol prohibition in the US, fashionable opinion was on the side of the smugglers. In addition, at least initially among the early users and even the general public, there was a widely held belief that cocaine was a non-addictive and harmless vice. In effect, it was considered a recreational and fashionable drug. Young professionals from lawyers and business types to movie stars and other celebrities were using it. It was upscale and widely accepted. With a lack of experience, like we had with drugs like heroin, it was glamorized to a high degree and thought to empower the user with energy and confidence.

I saw this first hand before I went to Colombia in 1984. At that time I had an office in the upscale

Georgetown area of Washington, DC. I remember how prevalent it was at parties and gatherings. Folks were even snorting up during the day in their offices or in the rest rooms of trendy restaurants and bars. It simply didn't carry the grimy loser image of other drugs—like heroin—that society associated with junkies shooting up in back alleys. After all, cocaine was pure white and usually snorted, not injected with dirty needles.

We had no long history of its impact on users and how addictive and destructive to lives it really was. So we gringos couldn't get enough. In a short period of time demand had skyrocketed, which powered the meteoric rise of the cartels in Colombia by providing them with billions of dollars. Any violence it spawned to the south was a Colombian problem, not ours.

Colombia shared that view, but from the other side of the coin. As Lewis Tambs, the Reagan Administration's ambassador to Colombia from 1983 to 1985, later noted, "Colombians didn't feel it was a Colombian problem, but a US problem because in spite of everything, they didn't use it. We did."

The Alignment of Cocaine and Leftist Politics

Tambs further noted that there was a sort of perverse pride within some quarters that drugs were destroying imperialism from within by its own excess. After all, if we didn't consume it, they would not produce it. In effect, they were throwing back in our faces our touted equation of supply and demand in a free market. The ambassador also observed that others took the notion even further and considered cocaine as a third world atomic bomb against imperialists. This idea of cocaine as a weapon of mass destruction against the US really appealed to Marxists like Fidel Castro and Daniel Ortega as they aligned themselves with the drug mafia.

From my travels and perspective, I detected an almost macho kind of pride among some Colombians that they were not weak enough to succumb to drug use. We were. It was an undertone of superiority they felt entitled to.

The truth, of course, is that it took its toll on both countries. Plus, it was beginning to impact politics in new ways that had a far reaching influence on the Americas as the relationship among drugs, politics, and revolution became closely intertwined. As you will see, for example, it suited the Reagan Administration to paint the drug cartels and leftists with the same brush, not just in Colombia but elsewhere as well.

Although a number of notable writers and other so called experts of that time dismissed any direct link between Colombian cartels and Marxists in the Americas, time would eventually reveal that Pablo Escobar and other drug lords were closely associated with the leftist rebels in the hemisphere. Various credible sources, for example, have indicated that $5 million was paid to the M-19 rebels to attack the Colombian Supreme Court in a bid to intimidate magistrates and destroy records and disrupt the extradition process.

While it's true that I possess no smoking gun in the form of embassy cables, wiretaps, or memos, I have the word of a guerrilla leader (Chapter 7), albeit uncorroborated with other rebels and, as you will see, the word of Colonel Ramirez, then the leader of Colombia's anti-narcotics forces.

As I came to understand it, the mafia-rebel partnership was an uneasy and troubled marriage of convenience. For instance, despite their collaboration, some guerrillas even tried to take over elements of the illegal drug business as the best way to finance their war against the Colombian government. They also resorted to kidnapping drug lord family members for ransom. It's important to also point out that their right-wing rivals, the paramilitaries, also undertook a similar campaign of violence.

Nonetheless, a key element of the story involves the cartels paying the rebels for protection against government forces. The Colombian government in turn increased its pressure on the cartels as this murky relationship began to emerge. Plus, it wasn't only confined to home grown Colombian revolutionaries. Pablo Escobar, for example, even started building ties with Daniel Ortega's Marxist Sandinistas in Nicaragua by helping to fund their rebel activities. He had the Central American government totally behind him because of the large sums of money he paid.

In addition to the Sandinistas, Castro was doing business with the cartel as Escobar continued to establish new drug routes in Cuba, Panama, and Nicaragua where he enjoyed a 6,000-foot airstrip on a military base. Likewise, Escobar also had a deal with Panamanian strongman General Manuel Noriega to allow the Medellin cartel to ship cocaine through Panama in exchange for large payments.

These relationships served to not only create a more robust drug pipeline to the US markets, but also to provide a place to escape to when the heat from authorities proved too much as well. They may, however, have helped shape public opinion of the day against the cartels. A photograph which surfaced, for example, showing Escobar helping Nicaraguan soldiers loading cocaine on a plane ultimately bound for the US, would come back to haunt him.

This was a time when the Reagan government, through Colonel Oliver North, was also running a covert operation in the opposite direction to smuggle in supplies to the Nicaraguan Contras in the Administration's attempt to topple the Sandinista's Marxist government. Any publicity to demonize the Sandinistas by showing their connection to Escobar and the illegal drug trade would have been very beneficial to the US.

Toward that end, on March 16, 1986, President Reagan went public and announced that all parents should be outraged to learn that top Nicaraguan government officials were deeply involved in drug trafficking aimed at American kids. The photo of Escobar helping to load drugs was also made public at that time.

In the end all the players had their weapons. The US had the power of extradition. The Colombians had the military and law enforcement muscle to put pressure on the mafia. The mafia had a no limits brand of violence that shocked and intimidated everyone.

The weapons of choice for the cartels included bribes, assassinations, and terror using both their own killers and contracting out other murders and assaults to leftist rebels like they did with the destruction of the Supreme Court. But one thing the players all had in common was that they all tried to use public opinion as a weapon.

Mafia leaders were well aware of the forces and factors arrayed against them. Moreover, they knew they had to battle to at least neutralize them if they were to survive. So the spiral of violence started to spin out of control as this potent brew of politics and police and military actions intensified pressure on the cartels. Their response was to put even more pressure on the system by taking wholesale terror to a new level, carrying out a staggering number of assassinations throughout Colombia. An estimated 3,500 were murdered during this period, including over 500 policemen in Medellin alone.

There were other groups, but the two most powerful cartels were based in Cali and Medellin, two main cities in Colombia. In the US, the Cali Cartel operated mostly out of New York, the Medellin Cartel concentrated on Miami, and they divided the city of Los Angeles. Medellin was the stronger of the two dominant cartels. Its undisputed godfather was Pablo Escobar. Under his leadership it's estimated that the Medellin cartel was earning $25 billion a year. As a measure of his success, by 1986 it was estimated that the Medellin Cartel had smuggled a whopping 60 tons of cocaine into the US. There were credible and persistent rumors at the time that he even offered to pay off the Colombian foreign debt of $8 billion if the government would terminate all extradition agreements with the US.

Even during these murderous times, under Escobar the Medellin cartel made extraordinary violence their special trademark. If you crossed him you were dead. I was told about some instances where his assassins actually cut off the testicles of those who had crossed Escobar, stuffed them into the victims mouth, and then stuffed the body into a barrel of chemicals as a warning to others. Although by all accounts he was deeply devoted to his own family, to Escobar it didn't matter if you were a man, woman, or child, he didn't hesitate to have you killed. And, if he had to kill the father he would kill the entire family, including parents, uncles, grandchildren, nephews and nieces.

Those were the times that the 1980s represented. They set the stage for what would be a conversation with the most memorable and fearless man I had ever interviewed.

A Quiet Interview with a Legend

Forty-seven year old Colonel Jaime Ramirez was at the forefront of the Colombian drug war. He was well respected and consulted not only in Colombia, but internationally, a living legend for both his integrity and his expertise. A DEA agent would later say Ramirez was Colombian to the bottom of his feet and very proud of his country. He further noted that the incorruptible Ramirez was a feisty, kickass type of guy who absolutely refused to be intimidated or scared off by either drug traffickers or corrupt politicians.

After I met him I could see why people thought so highly of him. I found him to be instantly likable with an air of quiet competence about him, not shy but certainly not chatty. I also found that he possessed a certain unpretentious courage and indefinable macho demeanor in the finest sense of the word.

It happened in early November, 1986, when Nydia and I were in Bogota staying with my in-laws for a few days. That's when my efforts to set up an interview with Ramirez finally bore fruit.

It began when the DEA called from the US Embassy with the message that Ramirez had agreed to meet with me. The rules were simple—no cameras or tape recorders, notes were fine. The meeting time was uncertain, but I was told to stand by and be ready when he would try and make himself available the following day. I asked my wife if she would translate. She agreed.

Early afternoon the next day we got another call and

were told to proceed to a certain part of El Dorado Airport on the edge of Bogota. We set off immediately. When we arrived at our destination we were met by two men in uniform. They gave us hard professional stares, but we were not physically searched. Few words were exchanged, but we were guided to a non-descript building well away from the main terminal.

We found ourselves standing next to a two story building with a few men armed with machine guns posted around the area. Our escort gestured to a metal ladder bolted to the side of the building. My wife and I exchanged glances, but did as directed. Once we reached the top of the building another man in uniform led us to a trapdoor in the flat roof, which he swung open.

Armed with a notebook and pen, we entered through the ceiling, coming down a ladder into an office with no doors and no windows. It had a desk angled in one corner and several chairs scattered about the room. It wasn't overly large, but not cramped either. It was cluttered with papers, but not messy. The walls were covered with various types of maps, some clearly of Colombia, others I presumed to be more detailed versions of specific areas.

Colonel Ramirez sat alone behind the desk dressed in olive green army fatigues. He had a clean shaven boyish face. He rose as we made our unusual entrance and I introduced myself and Nydia, explaining that she often translated for me. We all shook hands. He was courteous and professional, but didn't seem overly pleased see us. His first words both surprised and disappointed me because I thought they might signal an awkward interview.

"I don't normally meet with the press. In fact, I don't particularly like the reporters, especially foreigners."

"May I ask why?"

That's when he articulately laid it out without mincing words. He said, "I don't mean to be hostile, but let me be direct. They tend to place all of us in the same category. They all act like we are corrupt, incompetent or both, like we are a backward country. They view drugs as an exclusively Colombian problem. The only reason I agreed to talk with you is because I was told you are independent and really seeking to understand what is going on. Since I don't know you, though, I have no idea if that is the truth. I will tell you that if you do what some other journalists have done, it will be the last time we speak."

I assured him that it wasn't my intention to cast blame or to unnecessarily criticize, but to write stories that helped people understand the issue.

He seemed to consider that for a moment and then gestured for us to sit and politely invited me to ask whatever questions I wanted.

The first thing I did was comment on his office and extraordinary security.

"I have been threatened countless times." His demeanor was totally unflappable and calm.

"I also assume you have been offered bribes?"

"Yes, I could be a millionaire many times over. It's not me and it's not right. I have a great family and life. I don't need or want more."

"With so many killed, are you ever tempted to just say the hell with it, take the money and run and let someone else fight this fight?"

"I have a job to do and it's an important one. Someone has to do it. Colombia doesn't deserve this misery or this reputation and we have to do the right thing."

"Do you think the war on the cartels can be won?"

"We won't win it on our own that is for sure."

"Are you talking about resources from the US?"

"No, I'm not saying it's just a matter of receiving equipment and funding from your country, although that helps us strengthen our efforts."

"I'm not sure what you are saying. Moral support?"

"I said earlier that people, especially in the US, but Europe too, see us as the bad guys with the big problem. I don't argue that we have a handful of gangsters who have created a very dangerous climate. But, no matter how hard we try and stamp it out, how many we kill or arrest, there will always be others willing to supply illegal drugs as long as there are people willing to buy them. There is just too much money involved."

"So you are saying you view it equally as a US problem?"

"There are those who say this view is too simplistic, that Colombians are creating the demand. I say it's a problem on both ends and to say otherwise is to be dishonest."

"What do you think is the answer to the problem?"

"There are no easy or simple solutions. We must fight on both ends. We Colombians can work to cut off or reduce the supply, but we can't end the demand."

"Many writers and politicians have outright dismissed any connection between leftist rebels and the cartels. Books and articles have been written deriding this notion. They say such a connection is the invention of my government to further demonize socialists and communists."

"There is no doubt that the two are linked and there has been collaboration on some level."

"Can you be more specific?"

"There have been cases where cartels have funded leftist guerrillas for protection from us. But don't forget, it's not just them, but the right-wing paramilitaries, too."

"If I understand correctly, though, the guerrillas have kidnapped cartel family members for money, also."

"First you have to understand that the various leftist groups may have a common goal of intimidating or overthrowing the government in the name of creating some Marxist utopia, but they are all independent and under different leadership. They operate separately. These are not nice people. They are dangerous and violent and will do whatever they have to do to survive. That includes engaging in criminal activities to get money. They are not above trying to steal parts of the drug trade from the cartels. They are basically all criminals. That's what they do."

"So they sometimes help each other when it's convenient and steal from each other when they can?"

"You could say that."

"You said this war won't be won just on Colombian soil, but how do you think things are going?"

"As they earn more money and grab more power the cartels are becoming bolder, but we are fighting back hard. I have about 1700 men under my command and I can assure you they put not only their lives, but those of their families, too, on the line all the time. We win battles and we lose battles, but if we keep fighting we will be successful and win the war. At this moment things are very unstable and many people do not believe what I just said. And these skeptics are not just Colombians, but people in your country, too."

"How is your relationship with our DEA? Do you work closely together or like many law enforcement organizations, including those in my own country, each tends to operate in a vacuum?"

"I have nothing but praise for their agents. They have been very helpful and supportive and we work well together."

At that point he showed me some photographs of drug busts they had recently conducted, many with the help of DEA personnel. Then he told me about the DEA's role that led to Tranquilandia, the granddaddy bust of them all. He explained how thousands of gallons of chemicals, such as ether or acetone, are required to process cocaine. He noted that most of it came from the US and West Germany.

As a result, he went on to tell the following story of how the DEA had started to monitor large chemical buys in the US. When a buyer from Colombia showed up at a chemical plant in New Jersey wanting to pay cash for nearly two metric tons of ether, the DEA set up a sting operation, code named Operation Scorpion. Before the first barrels were shipped to Colombia, they were fitted with electronic tracking devices. Ultimately, the chemicals were traced to a dense jungle area in Colombia that was inaccessible by road.

Ramirez and his fellow law enforcement partners planned a raid on the location, never dreaming the magnitude of what would be found. On March 10th, 1984 police helicopters left at dawn. After reaching their destination they swooped in for the bust in an area called Tranquilandia (Tranquility-land). It was anything but tranquil or quiet. They initially found a fully equipped cocaine processing complex complete with an airfield and planes. It was producing an estimated 20 tons of cocaine a month, adding $12 billion dollars to Medellin Cartel accounts in less than two years.

Twelve similar complexes were found in the surrounding jungle, where drugs worth over an estimated billion dollars were destroyed, in total over 11 tons of cocaine. They also seized seven planes and over 10,000 drums of chemicals, all belonging to the

Medellin Cartel.

During the raid, police forces came under sniper fire, which Ramirez attributed to Marxists guerrillas being paid by Escobar to provide security. Nonetheless, the police prevailed. Chillingly, as Tranquilandia went up in smoke, they found a death list. Ramirez's name was on it, as was that of Rodrigo Lara Bonilla, the minister of justice and the colonel's boss.

It should be noted that at the time, Bonilla was one of few top ranking Colombian officials not afraid to take a hard line against drugs. For that, he was publically attacked by Escobar and his political allies as being a gringo puppet. Privately Escobar put out a contract on the minister's life. Ramirez said he was devastated because the man had a wife and three small children.

When this became known, according to Ramirez, Bonilla contacted Tambs, the American ambassador and asked for help, saying he didn't feel the Colombian government could any longer protect him. In response, the ambassador reportedly took steps for Bonilla to stay in the US, which was arranged through a wealthy American businessman who offered lodging and protection.

Despite this, Bonilla was murdered less than a month after Tranquilandia. Escobar was later indicted for the murder, but never stood trial. At that point, though, the Colombian government went after Escobar and his cartel with a vengeance, even raiding his hacienda. But the real godfather of cocaine was nowhere to be found.

He and his associates had already fled to their Marxists friends in Central America.

The only good to come out of Bonilla's death was that the view of the drug trade suddenly shifted from being either an exclusively American challenge or solely a Colombian issue to being a shared problem.

Ramirez further noted that while police operations in Tranquilandia were still underway, his brother contacted him and said that members of the Medellin cartel had come to his home. They had a message from Escobar they wanted passed along to Ramirez. It was simple. Cease all operations in Tranquilandia and withdraw his men and they would give him a multi-million dollar payoff.

When I asked what he did, he calmly responded that he had the place torched. His response spoke for itself and it was just as obvious he knew the risk he was taking. After all, Escobar had gone after other authorities literally hundreds of times, people like his friend and colleague General Miguel Maza, the chief of DAS. Miraculously Escobar had failed despite trying to have Maza killed on at least seven separate occasions.

Ramirez was direct and forthcoming with us. I believed we had good chemistry the way he had opened up. He agreed to meet with us again.

When it was over, we left the same way we came, through the ceiling. On the drive back to my in-laws, we talked about how impressed we were with the man and his dedication and integrity. Unfortunately, we would never see him again. The following images are a few photographs Ramirez gave me during our interview.

Torching part of a mountain cocaine complex.

A soldier adds to a blazing cache of drugs near a jungle lab.

Rifles and ammunition from Korea.

Burning a lab hidden in the jungle.

Tons of cocaine in flames in Tranquilandia.

A barrel of ether discovered in Tranquilandia from Operation Scorpion

A private airfield built by the cartel in Tranquilandia.

The End of a Hero

Because of the constant pressure, Ramirez was relieved of his post as head of the anti-narcotics force for a brief period of time at the end of 1985. During that time, Escobar sent a message to Ramirez, claiming to have cancelled the contract on his life because Ramirez was no longer directly involved in the Colombian government's efforts against the Medellin cartel. Escobar also said that he knew the colonel was only doing his job in his role in operations like Tranquilandia.

An honorable man of his word, Ramirez expected the same from others. Based on that and ignoring the fact that Escobar was one of the world's most notorious criminals, he must have believed the gangster would keep his promise. It's not clear if Escobar would have kept his part of the bargain if Ramirez had not returned again to head the anti-narcotics force of the national police after a brief respite.

After the message from Escobar about cancelling the contract, Ramirez believed it was safe to take his family away for a trip. On November 17th, 1986, the colonel set off with his family to drive from Medellin to Bogota. He was murdered on the highway when assassins in a red Renault pulled up beside his white Toyota and opened fire. His wife and two sons were wounded in the assault.

This happened less than two weeks after we had interviewed him. We were still in Bogota when we heard the shocking news of his murder on the evening news. Shaken and saddened, we returned to Pasto.

His widow, Helena, would later recall that the 17th was the first weekend in a very long time that the four of them had gone out as a family. She said it was about four in the afternoon when they set off for Bogota. She added that her and Jaime were talking about how they were getting to a stage in their lives when they should consider how they wanted to spend the rest of it. That's when it happened, gunfire and blood.

She said their car coasted to a stop and she got out to go around it and help her husband when she literally bumped into one of the killers. He was carrying a machine gun and she recounted asking him not to kill her. In her worst nightmare, he simply went over to Jaime and shot him again.

Afterwards, Escobar continued his murderous ways, including the killing of presidential candidate Luis Carlos Galan in August 1989. Galan was an outspoken opponent of the cartel. Years later in a strange and ironic turn of events, General Maza, the head of DAS at the time, was arrested when charges surfaced that his agency was complicit in the assassination of Galan.

I don't know the facts or if the allegations are true, but on the surface they make no sense to me since Escobar was behind the killing of Galan and he also tried to murder Maza no less than seven times. One thing this does illustrate, however, is the almost incomprehensible mosaic of threads that led in all directions and connected so many individuals and organizations during the dangerous decade that was 1980s Colombia.

As of late 2010, the matter is still ongoing with Maza under indictment. Among other things, he is accused of ordering Galan's protective guard force reduced; thus, ensuring that the assassin could get close to the presidential candidate.

Governments worldwide were shocked with the brutal murder of Galan. This resulted in an even greater effort by Colombian authorities to hunt down Escobar and his associates and they formed an elite force whose only job was to deal with the drug lord.

Escobar with 40 homes and refuges in Central America was a difficult target to hit and he managed to avoid them for a while. In addition, his terror tactics briefly proved effective when Colombia banned extradition in 1991. The coalition of enemies arrayed against him, however, were relentless and growing. They included a loose alliance among the Colombian police and army, the DEA, right-wing paramilitary killers, and his rivals in the Cali cartel, not to mention any surviving relatives of people he had murdered.

Finally and fittingly, on December 2, 1993, he died the same violent death he had visited on so many others when Colombian national police found him hiding in a middle class neighborhood in Medellin with his bodyguard, Alvaro de Jesus Agudelo, also known as El Limon (the lemon). The two fugitives had climbed out a window and started running across the roof tops in their efforts to escape when they were gunned down. Escobar suffered gunshots to the leg, torso, and a fatal slug in his ear.

9

ROAD TRIPS, BORDER CROSSINGS & CARNIVALS

In the mid-1970s, well before we moved there, my wife and I started to fly to Pasto to visit her older sister Mary and her husband. Since it's high in the Andes with peaks and crests everywhere you can imagine the challenge the people of Pasto faced when trying to establish an airport.

Naturally, their answer was to build one on the top of a mountain, which made for some interesting dynamics. I vividly remember the first time we landed there. I could hear the pitch of the jet engines change to a deeper whine as we drifted down and the pilot announced that we should all buckle up for landing. As I peered out the window, all I saw were mountains and steep walled valleys and I wondered where in the hell we were going to land.

The plane continued to slow and level off and I knew we were getting close to landing, but it was not clear where. It was still a long way down. At the last minute the edge of a runway appeared, much like the deck of an aircraft carrier. We hit the tarmac and careened down it. The engines roared and the pilot braked finally coming to an abrupt stop.

There were no jet ports at that time so they wheeled a set of stairs to the door for passengers to disembark from the big plane. Once on the airstrip I glanced at the end of the runway we had been racing down and saw nothing but open space. This always fascinated me and I came to have great respect for the pilots who landed there. They were very good.

When my wife would fly alone I would stand in the small terminal and watch as her plane accelerated from the far end of runway toward the other side. The plane would literally sail off the end of the strip and disappear. Then seconds later it would reemerge as it took flight.

Although I flew often around the country (when the airport wasn't closed because clouds were sitting on top of it obscuring all visibility), my most memorable and event filled trips were by car. My main run was the thousand kilometers from Pasto to Bogota on the Pan-American Highway, but I also drove to the coast and other departments.

Like most countries, Colombia honors international drivers licenses, which at that time were a gray passport-sized document issued here in the States by the American Automobile Association. It had the driver's photo, some rules printed in several languages, and an expiration date. If you got stopped, you showed your AAA license and passport.

It was valid for one year. I used mine for over three years, not out of disrespect for the law, but because of the logistics involved to get it renewed in the US. The first year when it expired I couldn't get to the States so I renewed it myself.

I had a paper embosser from the Montgomery County Maryland Library system (it's still a mystery to me where I got it). It featured a circular design with the county seal on it. I simply drew a single line through the expired date, wrote in a new date and embossed over it. (Like government types all over the world, Colombian officials love stamps and seals on documents.) It passed inspection on numerous occasions. And, I must say, I got sort of a perverse kick out of it.

Since I was constantly being stopped on the road, the license became an important document to have and I was always armed with my license, passport, and camera when I set off in my car.

At that time both the authorities and the leftist guerrillas would pick lonely stretches of road and set up road blocks. The problem was as you approached these barricades you couldn't tell if they were being manned by the good guys or the bad guys. Either way, they almost always consisted of a group of heavily armed men surrounding a wooden saw horse, a pile of rocks, or a stack of brush in order to block the road.

On one of my early trips from Pasto to the capital, I got my first taste of what it was like. I had departed from home alone in the morning and somewhere between Pasto and Popayan, the next city on the highway, I came to a blockade. It turned out to be Colombian national police or soldiers; I wasn't sure except that they were official.

Traffic was sparse and I pulled up and stopped. They made me get out of the car and inspected it and my passport and license. There was the usual curiosity on their part about what a gringo was doing in a remote part of Southwestern Colombia, but I was soon on my way. Within a few kilometers I came upon another barricade manned again by a group dressed in the same olive green uniforms of the police and the military. I thought it was odd, but had no choice but to stop.

I went through the same routine, not fully understanding the situation at that point. After all, even if they are the police, they simply do not show you any identification so you are left to guess whether they are legitimate or not. Unfortunately, in this case, they were guerrillas. They questioned me for over an hour, stripping me of my camera and all my documents. I believe their intent was to kidnap me. As it turned out, though, all they did was take all my money.

I convinced them that I wasn't the enemy, just your average writer reporting the news. I also made a convincing case that I was not a wealthy person and not really worth taking. But to this day I believe what finally swung things in my favor were the photos of my family in my wallet and the fact that I was married to a Colombiana. I told them I was not here to write negative stories or take sides but merely write about events, people, and things. I emphatically pointed out that Colombia was routinely on the receiving end of bad press and one of my goals was that no matter what I was writing about, to highlight the positive.

Like many things that happened to me at that time, it all seemed a little surreal, like I was watching it happen to someone else. It would be a total lie for me to say, however, that I wasn't scared. My legs were definitely shaky and my breathing was shallow, but I survived. It would be one of the numerous times I would be stopped by both government and rebel forces. That's just the way it was then. I never really got used to it, but I did get very good at telling my standard story about who I was and what I was doing.

Those unpredictable blockades were one of the reasons I hesitated to travel with my family by car in remote areas. After all, the roads themselves were dangerous enough without exposing my loved ones to unnecessary peril.

They were not generally dual highways, but two lane roads. Usually there were no guard rails or warning signs and driving off a mountain was a realistic possibility if you weren't careful. There were no speed limits and even if there had been there was no highway patrol to enforce them. Your speed was limited by the roads themselves, which followed the spectacularly beautiful topography. There were no lines on the roads to indicate the center or the no passing zones. Cars, buses, and trucks all jockeyed for road rights in a sort of mechanized kabuki dance. You learned the unwritten rules and you also instinctively memorized the curves and straight stretches of the roads you traveled or you risked life and limb.

Looking back, it's a wonder that anyone could build some of those roads at all. From Pasto northward, the Andes split into three chains, separated by deep valleys. The Western Cordillera has five peaks over 13,000 feet high. The Central Cordillera is even higher with six snowcapped peaks that rise as high as 19,000 feet in the sky. It's flanked by the country's two major rivers, the Cauca and the Magdalena. The longest range is the Eastern, which basically runs up through Colombia and into Venezuela. In effect, the ranges divide Colombia into the highlands, the coastal lowlands, and the eastern plains and the jungles of the Amazon. I drove in all these areas, but spent most of my time in the mountains.

One ever present group traversing the country was the truckers. They were extraordinary in both their driving skills and their mechanical expertise. I thought of them at the time as iron men driving tin trucks. You could always count on them to lend a hand and tools in fixing a mechanical problem or other emergency.

There were very few truck stops in rural areas at

that time. In fact, they were almost non-existent. If a trucker broke down, though, they simply whipped out their tools and fixed the problem, often improvising when needed parts were not available. They were truly talented and tough.

Given that the mountain roads did not have emergency lanes to accommodate breakdowns, they would walk back up the highway and stack a pile of stones on the road or cut some brush and use that to warn other drivers that there was a disabled vehicle ahead. Then they would proceed to deal with the mechanical problem while their truck was in the road. Seeing a pile of stones worked great during daylight hours, but I often drove at night and learned to be very vigilant, ever on the lookout for signs that one of the behemoths might be blocking the way ahead.

The most thrilling part of the drive to Bogota was something called "La Linea." It was where the highway crested the Central Cordillera, just past the city of Armenia. It was like riding a roller coaster when the car chugs up the steep incline then plunges down the other side, except that there were some significant curves thrown in for good measure. As if that wasn't adrenaline inducing enough, the sheer altitude ensured that the road was often covered in clouds, which produced the thickest fog-like conditions one can imagine. But not all of my travel adventures where by car.

Illegal Border Crossing

To live and write in Colombia as a US citizen required me to obtain a resident visa. When I got the visa I didn't realize it also required something else. That is, every time I wanted to travel outside Colombia I had to get what they called a paz y salvo. This necessitated going to a lot of government offices, like DAS, and proving I wasn't wanted by the police or that I didn't owe the Colombian government any money. If I didn't get the document, I literally couldn't get out of the country.

In the spring of 1987, I had an unexpected opportunity to interview a venerable Catholic Cardinal for a story, but I had two problems. I would have to travel to Quito, Ecuador, to conduct the interview; and, given the deadline, I didn't have time to go through all the bureaucratic hoops to get a paz y salvo for the trip.

I knew I could drive to Ipiales on the Colombian side of the border, walk across the bridge connecting the two countries to Tulcan, Ecuador, and catch the daily flight to Quito. Although I would have preferred to spend the night in Quito, I also knew that if I could make the return flight later in the day it would essentially be a day trip. So, I made the decision to go for it.

I wanted Armando along to ensure that I got the translation right and we set off for Ipiales. We parked and walked to the border crossing, which was basically a bridge connecting the two countries. There was a steady stream of pedestrians and cars crossing in both directions under the watchful eye of officials at each end of the span. We joined in the procession of pedestrians.

As we passed by the uniformed Colombian officials, one yelled at me. I cursed my bad luck but had to comply and stopped. He looked at my passport and chastised me for not having the right paperwork to leave the country. I explained I planned to return later that evening and didn't think I needed it. This, of course, was not strictly true, but nonetheless I feigned ignorance. He made it clear, however, that without the paperwork he would not allow me to pass.

We retreated to a spot where a vendor was selling coffee and small meat kabob type snacks to evaluate our options. As we sat sipping coffee and munching our food we watched the action at the head of the bridge. We were almost ready to turn around and go home when we saw the guy who had given us grief leave the area, apparently on break.

Before I could even express my thoughts, Armando was already studying my face and shaking his head, telling me I was crazy. In the end we made a successful break for it and were able to get to the airport and catch the flight.

We arrived in Quito only to learn that the elderly cardinal was sick and the interview had been postponed until further notice. So, we promptly turned around and went back to the airport for the return flight to Tulcan. I was a little apprehensive and we decided to linger on the Ecuadorian side until well after dark before we attempted to cross back into Colombia. We almost made it.

Reaching the end of the bridge, I heard a loud voice calling to me. At first I pretended not to know who he was talking to, but the man would not be deterred. It was the same official from my morning skirmish. He was very excited and angry as he approached me, demanding my passport. I looked for Armando, but he was gone. Another border official joined the first. There was a rapid stream of Spanish. I knew I was in trouble. All doubt was removed when they each grabbed an arm, frog marched me to a vehicle, and tossed me in. I was transported to a nearby building. It happened in a blur and I found myself alone in a filthy jail cell.

I wondered where in the devil Armando was in my time of need. I would learn later that as he saw the trouble at the bridge shaping up he had quietly and wisely blended into the crowd, lingering to watch the action while he bought a pack of cigarettes from a street vendor.

I can control my emotions in tight enclosed spaces, but I have a strong claustrophobic streak in me and it was all I could do to keep it together. I was alone, so in typical gringo fashion (I know my rights...), the first thing I did was yell and demand to make a call. This was all met with silence.

I started to hyperventilate. My breath came in gulps despite my best efforts to remain calm. So, I focused all my energy on my surroundings. The walls were covered with names and graffiti, most of which I couldn't understand.

Along with my other possessions they had taken my

The spectacular sanctuary church Las Lajas built in chasm near
Ipiales on the Colombian-Ecuadoran border.

watch. I quickly lost all sense of time. I started to play
mental games, doing math problems in my head, trying
to recall passages from books, and whatever else I could
think of to distract myself from my predicament.

At one point an older man, rounded the corner and
looked at me. I tried to talk to him, but my efforts were
met with a stare and he disappeared. I sat on a cot with
a thin, disgusting, foul smelling mattress. Agonizing
and wondering if anyone knew where I was, I played
the possibilities over and over in my mind. I convinced
myself that Armando must know, even though it had
all happened so fast I didn't even have the chance to

exchange a glance with him. Still I kept telling myself that he must know. This thought played through my mind in an endless loop. It was my only source of hope.

I tried to rationalize the situation by guessing that at some point they would have to take me before a judge or some other senior official and I could plead my case. I really hadn't committed any major crime, or at least I didn't think I had. I tried to doze off sitting up, but never did. I yelled some more, but got no response from my captors.

After what would turn out to be over five hours, I heard loud voices and a commotion down the dingy hall that fronted the cells. Moments later Armando and the Colombian consul to Ecuador appeared before my cell with the older man I had briefly seen earlier.

I was never so happy to see anyone in my life. The cell was unlocked. I was led down the passageway and was able to retrieve my things. We finally spilled outside the building and into the cool night air. Oddly enough I was never asked to sign any papers so maybe they hadn't officially processed me with whatever crime they intended to charge me. I don't know and don't really care, except for the curiosity and wondering if somewhere in some dusty office cabinet there is a file on me.

I was giddy with relief when I walked free with my friends, but one dark thought kept intruding on my sense of well-being. That is, if I ever really was a criminal I would rather be shot than caged. (The irony of this sentiment I shared with Pablo Escobar was not lost on me.)

Getting sprung was the result of my good fortune of living in the Palermo neighborhood of Pasto. That fact alone was the reason. My neighbors in the upscale section included a senator, the mayor, the governor, and the consul. I knew all of them or had socialized with them at parties and other gatherings.

On the drive home, Armando recounted the events that led up to my release. He told me that after I was snatched, he had quietly left the area, retrieved the car, and driven back to Pasto. There he quickly briefed the first of our prominent neighbors he could find and came back to the rescue.

It was late. Feeling a little frazzled, I thanked them and went home and gave my wife and kids a big hug. I then poured a stiff drink and caught up my journal and reflected on the whole brief episode.

In putting things in perspective, I knew they thought I was an arrogant gringo by apparently disrespecting them and their laws. I really couldn't blame them. (Even though I viewed my transgression as more a matter of expedience and necessity rather than just thinking I was special in any way.) If the roles had been reversed, though, I suspect I would have thought the same thing. I had the nagging feeling then, as I do now, that my actions confirmed the kind of behavior that infuriates Colombians and helps reinforce the stereotype that outsiders think they are special and the rules don't apply to them.

Carnival—the Days of Black, White & Water

If there is one thing Colombians really know how to do it is to enjoy a great lifestyle. They know how to relax, relieve stress, and party. For the most part they don't drown in bills, papers, junk mail, kids' taxi duty overload (think soccer practice, swim meets, and study groups) and the million other little things that seem to clutter our lives here in the US. They love music, dancing, and socializing. In fact, Colombian music is world renown. I don't know of anyone who hears a Cumbia who can resist the urge to dance or at least tap their foot to the infectious beat. These things all come together in grand style once a year throughout the country in the form of carnivals in various cities, including Pasto.

The Black and White Carnival is generally held the first week in January in Pasto. It's one of the most ancient carnivals in the Americas. I have been told somewhat conflicting stories about its origin by various historians and history enthusiasts. Some say it started in 1607 when there was a slave rebellion in the department of Antioquia that made the authorities panic. Others say the event stems from the black population of the department of Cauca, who demanded a day off in which they were truly free. No matter, the king of Spain finally conceded and the carnival was born.

Allegedly, when the news reached the black

population they flocked into the streets and danced. Whites joined them and started to blacken their faces with coal or grease in empathy. This enthusiastic celebration was supposedly brought to Pasto in the mid-1800s. One thing certain is that all seem to agree it commemorates a time in which African slaves were given a free day when they could unconditionally express their happiness and love of life. Their masters showed their approval by painting their faces black and the slaves responded by putting chalk white powder on theirs.

The prelude to the days of black and white is the Castaneda Family Parade. This procession evokes the legend that years ago the people of Pasto invited a special family, called the Castaneda family, to their feasts. Later, to commemorate the arrival of this family a large group of residents would dress up in period clothes and parade through the streets to take the spectators back to the earlier times. It's truly an enchanted day of celebration and music and sharing laughs and drinks with whomever you happen to be next to in streets that are overflowing with thousands of people.

During my holiday visits to my wife's family, I had been enjoying the wonderful carnivals in Pasto for years before I moved there. But this unique time starts even before the official carnival kicks off in January. It begins with the day of the Holy Innocents the end of December. From there carnival can be broken up into the day of water, the day of blacks, and the day of whites.

For many reasons, including a climate where the average temperature is barely 55 degrees Fahrenheit, it is my understanding that the water day is no longer practiced. Back then, though, it was a day of water tricks and practical jokes. If you were walking in the street it was very likely that someone would drop a water balloon or a bucket of water on your head from a balcony. Or just run up to you and soak your clothes. People laughed good naturedly and often responded in kind. It was just accepted, regardless of who you were or how you were dressed.

We used to get my sister- and brother-in-law and the kids and head out in his old Land Rover. The back would be filled with containers of cold water. We would cruise the streets looking for unsuspecting victims. We often ended up getting in epic water fights with total strangers. As we opened the doors of the Rover to deliver our water bombs, we were also the recipients of buckets of water being tossed into the vehicle. Many others would do the same thing and the streets were filled with roving water warriors in trucks, carts and on foot. It was all in good fun and when we all ran out of water, strangers and family alike would all share a laugh and a few shots of aquardiente to ward off the cold.

(I should note that since the 1600s when the King of Spain, fearing it led to moral decay, tried to ban it, aguardiente has been Colombia's beloved national drink. Crystal clear, it is made from sugar cane and laced with anise. It is not a sipping drink and is served by the shot and downed in a single gulp. It knows no class boundaries.)

Soaking wet, cold, and excited we would then head home for a refill of water, perhaps some dry clothes and venture back out again. Indeed, this day was marked by city-wide water fights and pranks. It changed the whole mood of the city for one day as adults acted like kids and kids acted like... well, like kids.

This ushered in the day of the blacks. We would dress in old clothes, a bottle of aquardiente in hand and venture downtown. The streets would be filled with people, most with a small jar of black makeup. We would approach our fellow partiers and slather the black grease-like substance on their faces, unless they were already sufficiently smeared. Others would do the same to us. We were like kids chasing each other around the streets trying to turn everyone black.

The closer to the main plaza you went, the bigger the crowds and the rowdier the action. Orchestras would be playing music in a sort of choreographed chaos. Tempers did not flare. We were all there to share the fun and enjoy the moment. I always saw many people I knew and many strangers became friends on that day.

This would be followed by the day of the whites and the grand parade. This incredible parade is characterized by a great procession of incredible floats, which stretched several kilometers long. Made by extraordinarily talented artisans and consisting of elaborate, colorful, larger than life figures and scenes depicting everything from mountains to Amazon themes, they rival floats found in any such parade in the world. It becomes a fascinating, joyous melding and display of cultures. These enormous floats are so large and intricate that it takes the entire year to make them.

The day of the whites was essentially a repeat of the day of blacks except that people throw white power or smear white cosmetics on each other. Like its black counterpart, I remember towards the end of the day all you could see were people's eyes as they danced and shared drinks, often using the top of the bottle as a makeshift shot glass.

(Please note for those purists among you that I may have the timing of the events slightly out of sequence since I am relying on my memory to recount these magical celebrations. These were generally not events I recorded in my journal.)

I never tired of the carnivals. Even though they were young at the time, my daughters also recall those celebrations as times when the word joy took on its full meaning.

I understand from family and friends that the personality of the city has changed somewhat over the years as it has grown. Although I still frequently spend time in Colombia, especially Bogota and its surrounding countryside, I cannot say for sure how profound the changes are since I have not visited Pasto for a long time.

It is also my understanding that carnival is no longer held in the streets. Perhaps it grew too large and boisterous, but the government has built a special plaza for the celebrations. I cannot imagine carnival in a confined space like a stadium because for me partying in the streets was part of the unique, spontaneous, and magical time that was carnival. Perhaps that is why I have never felt compelled to return for carnival. I know times change, but that's just how I feel. I am happy, though, that the generations who followed still keep this wonderful tradition alive in some form.

10
BUILDING A HOME ON A VOLCANO

The owner of the house we originally leased wanted to sell the property. We liked the house and considered buying it, but in the end we decided to build our own home. Consequently, we moved out of the house on Calle 39 in the Palermo neighborhood and into a large apartment a couple of blocks over on 41st. It was the top unit in a three story building and the view was idyllic and impressive. From the rear windows you could see the long green slope, with its patchwork of different colored fields, which ascended toward the summit of the Galeras volcano.

We had a family room toward the back of apartment. One wall featured a long wall unit containing books, a stereo, and TV. At both ends of the wooden cabinet were large hanging plants in baskets suspended from the ceiling. The opposite wall was a sofa and chairs.

It was on a Sunday evening. The girls were in bed.

Downtown Pasto, 1985.

The housekeeper was in her room off the kitchen terrace. My wife and I were alone, sitting on the couch watching TV. Suddenly the couch seemed to jump about half a foot off the floor. Startled, I turned to her and asked what she was doing. She looked back at me and said she wasn't doing anything. Then we noticed the hanging plants swinging wildly.

At the same time there was low rumble that could only be described as a deep mournful moan. It grew louder like an approaching freight train. The building shook violently. The lights flickered. The walls and ceiling of the concrete structure seemed to literally ripple as the earth moved and the first of many shock waves passed though the building.

We dashed into the girls' room and scooped them up into our arms. A few seconds of stillness were followed by the rumble and the shaking again. Without hesitation we headed for the front of apartment and the main door. (Most entry doors in Colombia contain a deadbolt that must be locked or unlocked from both sides by a key.)

Our door consisted of a thick wooden slab with an elaborate wrought iron grill over it. The deadbolt was secure and the key was not in the lock. For an instant I panicked as I searched my pockets and tried to remember what I had done with the key. By this time the building was shaking even more violently. After what seemed an interminable period of time, we found the key and hurried down the stairs carrying the girls.

I remembered that experts advise people to get under a solid structure, like a doorway, during an earthquake and not to rush into the street where you are likely to be injured or killed by falling debris. At that moment I didn't care. I wanted to be free of the terror of the shaking structure. So, along with our neighbors, we rushed into the street to take our chances. This pattern was repeated throughout the night as we waited for dawn.

There was a wonderful older couple who lived in the apartment below ours. They graciously invited us to sip some sherry and pass the time with them as we waited for first light. This worked out well not only because we welcomed the companionship, but because with each new tremor we were closer to the main door of the building and the relative freedom of the street.

This happened in March 1987 and by the light of day we learned that a 7.0 magnitude earthquake had killed approximately 1,000 people, 4,000 were missing and 20,000 homeless. The most extensive damage occurred in Ecuador with far less extending up into our region of southwest Colombia.

Although Pasto had escaped the brunt of the quake, the tremors continued for days. One image that remains vivid in my memory was the view of the slope on the side of the massive volcano that faced Pasto. At one point during the aftershocks I saw the slope literally ripple as though someone had snapped the end of a long green rug and the rolling wave traveled the entire length of it. I can still hear the haunting moan as the shock reverberated toward the city.

It's unnatural, of course, to have the ground continually shift beneath your feet. At more than one point during those days and nights I would have gladly paid for a helicopter to lift me up so things would stop moving by suspending me in the relative stability and stillness of the air.

As time passed and the memory of the shaking ground faded, we pressed on with the business of life and the way ahead, although it served to remind us of the volatile nature of the country itself and the explosive nature of our physical environment. Events were becoming increasingly cumulative as the warning from Jaime, the murder of Ramirez, the quake, and other factors continued to add to my mental list of troubling signs. Starting with things that impacted our dreams to build a house, it was subsequent factors, though, which finally caused us to alter our plans.

I should have known better. Volcanic activity and earthquakes go hand in hand, especially in the ring of fire. That is, the line of volcanos that march up western South America through Central America and Mexico and the continental US to Alaska and around and down through Japan and Asia. So, in hindsight it was a very foolish decision even though I was incredibly lucky in the way it ultimately turned out.

I still wonder what we had been thinking when we bought a parcel of beautiful land nestled up against the base of the Galeras Volcano. To be sure, the soil was black and fertile after thousands of years of being periodically nurtured by the volcano. The grass was lush and there were magnificent stands of eucalyptus trees that filled the air with a wonderful aromatic scent.

Our close friends, Patricia and Jorge, were just down the road where they had established the best school in that entire region of the country. In fact, their Montessori school was probably the best grade school I had ever seen anywhere.

In my mind Galeras was extinct. After all, it had been silent for many decades. Later I would recall the words of a German volcanologist I talked to when I was researching the Nevado del Ruiz volcano in the aftermath of the destruction it wreaked on the city of Armero, killing 23,000 people. He said, "There is no such thing as an extinct volcano. They may be dormant for a time, even centuries, but they are never dead."

There was already a magnificent old Spanish style home, complete with solarium and indoor pool, in the vicinity of our lot. In fact, it was the owner who had sold us the land. After we bought it land prices in the area skyrocketed. Conventional wisdom was, "If this gringo is buying land here he must know something we don't." They couldn't have been more wrong. We simply wanted a beautiful and peaceful location out of the city to build our dream house. Regardless, the parcels of land eventually sold out and it became an exclusive area even before any homes were built.

We hired workers to clear the lot in preparation of breaking ground. An access road was developed and a power line and transformer were installed to provide electricity to the development. We had a design in mind and sent to the States for the architectural drawing for the big English country-style house we wanted with lots of wood, brick, stone, and glass. I did some research on builders and talked to the man I wanted to do the work. I also researched wood companies to find such items as the structural beams and wooden planking we would need.

I thought things were shaping up quite nicely. The first sign of problems came not from the volcano, but as the result of a strike, which made it impossible to buy the brick we needed for the foundation. I wasn't worried, though. It would surely end and we would press on. In the meantime, we waited expectantly for the house plans to arrive by mail. Weeks literally turned into months. We contacted the source of the drawings and were told they had been sent. More time passed and my frustration was reaching new levels.

We found out later that the drawings had indeed been sent much earlier, but had been inexplicably ignored, lying forgotten for months in the corner of a postal facility in Bogota. By this time we had lost some of our eagerness for the project.

Whatever enthusiasm remained disappeared in an instant on New Year's Eve with one phone call. Early in the day my mother-in-law had gone to the market to shop for items for her New Year's Eve party. With no warning she suffered a massive stroke and went into a coma. My wife rushed to Bogota and I stayed home to take care of our daughters. The doctor said it was impossible to say if or when she would regain consciousness. It could be an hour, a day, a month, or never. My wife and her siblings were distraught, remaining by her bedside at the hospital.

My mother-in-law never woke and within 24 hours she was gone. The news devastated the family. Her death was a time of deep reflection for us. It also served to

Pasto with the Galeras volcano looming in the background.

highlight our failure to get construction underway and to rethink the safety of our family given other issues, such as the warning by Jaime.

We had been in Colombia for three years and had planned to stay for at least eight to give the girls a good opportunity to enjoy their cousins and other family members and develop a lasting appreciation for one side of their culture and heritage. It was then we started to discuss forgetting the house and returning to the US. Once we did, it didn't take long for us to make a difficult final decision.

The volcano was silent and still, but little did we know how quickly that would change. The school year was coming to a close so the timing seemed right if we were going to do it. We decided that I would go back to the states and start to prepare everything since we would have to sell most of our furniture and car in Colombia because of the prohibitive cost of shipping it home. We needed everything, from a place to live to transportation.

My wife stayed behind to wrap things up. At first I didn't want to leave her and the girls behind for fear of their security. We reached the consensus, though, that without me in the picture everyone would be safe.

Within a couple of months we were reunited in the States and started to establish a normal routine for ourselves and the girls. We still owned our land in Colombia, but we put the word out that we were interested in selling. One day a man called us from New York City and said his brother lived in Nariño and wanted to buy it. It turned out to be perfect for us. We arranged to have the paperwork done in Colombia and were paid in dollars without the hassle of trying to convert the money and repatriate it to the US.

My youngest brother-in-law, Luis Eduardo, and his family were still living in Pasto. A few months after we sold he called and said that Galeras had started to rumble and smoke. The volcano then became increasingly active as time progressed. It was then that we fully realized how fortunate we had been. Many of the beautiful houses that had been built in our old neighborhood after we left were threatened and damaged. Eventually they all had to be abandoned. If we had built, we would have lost the house. I felt sorry for the others who did lose their homes, with even the value of their land plunging to almost nothing.

Like many things that happened to me during my journey in Colombia, it was purely serendipitous that it didn't have disastrous consequences for us. This has enhanced my belief that we can usually only appreciate the force fate has on our lives when we reflect on the nature of our existence. In doing so I have come to realize that I lived there at a time that was characterized by the alignment of a series of unusual events in an extraordinary environment with an almost random force that seemed to guide many of my conscious and subconscious actions and decisions.

As my sister, Pauline, would say, "Planning is great, but too often it's just pure luck how things work out." She is also fond of saying, "It's better to be lucky than good." She will get no argument from me.

11
THE FAMILY

Nothing I write about Colombia would be complete without acknowledgment of the role played by the incredible family I married into almost forty years ago. They gave us the moral support, love, and friendship that helped us establish and sustain a new life.

Before I share a few mini-tales about them, though, it's important to understand a little about who they are. With eight sisters and two brothers, the family is defined by strong character and full of unique characters as well. The oldest and youngest are males with the sisters in between. I am, of course, somewhat biased when it comes to this wonderful bunch of folks.

But on a purely objective level, I believe they are more the norm of Colombian families, rather than the exception. They are generous, gregarious, with a deep appreciation for family and a lifestyle based on living the life we have to the fullest as it comes day by day.

Colombian families tend to be larger when compared to those in the US. They also tend to be closer (not always in a geographic sense) in terms of their interactions and relationships with each other. Depending on the situation, they can be headed by either a male or female, but there tends to be a strong central figure the others look up to and seek advice from on many matters.

For us it was my mother-in-law. When she invited you for holiday parties or a Sunday lunch, you came. Her demeanor was such that she engendered both the love and respect of the family. When things got tough and you needed encouragement or advice, she was there.

After she passed on, this mantle fell to my father-in-law, a remarkable man in his own right. Although slender and wiry, he was unbelievably tough in a physical sense. He owned a wrought iron company that made everything from patio furniture to window frames and decorative balcony railings. He loved his factory and never hesitated to get his hands dirty, but he was old school formal and I never saw him without a coat and tie. It didn't matter if he was coming from the shop or going on a picnic in the countryside, that's how he dressed. He had a contagious laugh and the sense of humor and timing of a professional comedian. In fact, he looked somewhat like George Burns.

His first love, though, was music. A talented guitar player he was instrumental in one of his grandsons teaching music and becoming a member of the Colombian national symphony, as well as the inspiration for other musically talented family members. After he retired from his business you could seldom find him without a guitar in his hands. Although his hands were large and tough, they could skillfully skim over the frets and strings and create pure classical Spanish guitar music.

He was part of various bands and groups and loved to play for parties and in fine restaurants. In a quiet moment with me, he once joked that the worst part about getting old was the size of his band as he outlived his contemporaries. He said, "I started out with an orchestra, then with time we became quintet, then a quartet, then a trio, then a duo, and now I'm a solo." Although he enjoyed his cigarettes and the occasional glass of whisky or aguardiente, he lived a robust life, passing away at age 94.

Like my mother-in-law, his memory never leaves me and I still laugh and remember fondly how he touched my life.

I hope the following smattering of vignettes and memories help capture their spirit as well as the joy, love, excitement, zest, and sense of humor the family continues to bring to life and to each other. I believe they also capture the unique perspective on life that is prevalent in Colombia, especially in large close families. Although they face the same pressures, for example, financial, health, and work stress, that families everywhere face, their fundamental lifestyle is more relaxed and more optimistic.

Striving to be a Macho Man

In the mid-1970s, I went to my first real family party when my youngest brother-in-law, Luis Eduardo, graduated from high school. My in-laws had a house north of Bogota in a rural setting. For the occasion they had moved all of the furniture out of the large living room to accommodate my father-in-law's musicians and dancing.

It was a family affair and in attendance along with aunts, uncles, cousins, nephews, and nieces, were five of my brothers-in-law. I was meeting most of them for the first time since my wife and I had married in the States and many family members could not be in attendance for the ceremony. The festivities started late, about 9 pm. I found myself standing close to the entrance to the kitchen in a circle conversing with my brothers-in-law.

Every 20 or 30 minutes a maid would appear carrying a silver tray with crystal shot glasses full of aguardiente for us. We would click glasses, toast each other, and toss them back in a single gulp. As I drank mine, I noticed that they would all somewhat mischievously peer at me to see my reaction. As the evening progressed it dawned on me that they wanted to get the gringo a little drunk and see how I would react. It wasn't malicious, just a macho thing. That's when I decided to be a bit mischievous myself and I formulated a plan to turn the tables on them.

Excusing myself to use the bathroom, I stopped by

the kitchen and talked to the maid. I explained that from that point on she should fill my glass with water and discretely set it slightly apart on the tray when offering the drinks. She understood immediately and smiled. As the guest she always offered me my drink first, so there was little danger that I wouldn't select the right shot glass.

The evening wore on and we danced, but always returned to our spot for our group drink. As the hours passed, my brothers-in-law faded one by one and drifted away. By early in the morning (I think it was about 6 AM) the party was still going with some folks dancing and others talking. At this point it was just Hector, my oldest brother-in-law, and I in our little circle. He kept looking at me a little blurry eyed and shaking his head, although as always his speech was deliberate and articulate. Something he prided himself on. Over the years I almost never heard him use profanity. That night (actually morning), though, he finally looked at me and said with some admiration, "You are one tough son of a bitch."

I smiled and raised my glass in a toast to him and told him I would take that as a compliment. He said I should. I was never challenged again by this group of great guys as to whether or not I was macho. It wasn't until some years later that I revealed the secret of that night. They all laughed. By that time, of course, we had all become close friends.

Doctor Who?

Farmers in Colombia often use natural fertilizer, in lieu of the chemical variety. As a result, eating salad or raw vegetables washed in tap water or drinking unfiltered water can cause you to get small parasites in your system. They are treatable and while painful are certainly not life threatening.

In my early travels I was not always as careful as I should have been with what I ate and drank. During one of my first trips in the 1970s, I became very sick with significant stomach distress. My wife and mother-in-law instantly gave me the diagnosis of amoebas. I was further informed that it might pass through my system in a day or two. It didn't. Within a few days I could not venture more than a few feet from a bathroom.

We all agreed that I needed to see a doctor and get a prescription for the condition, but since we were outside the city no definite plans were made. Then Stellita, one of my sisters-in-laws, said she knew a doctor and would call him. I don't remember if he stopped by or just had the right pills delivered, but within a short time I had medicine.

I received the pills gratefully and took the first one. The only extraordinary thing that I noticed about them was that they were huge. I mean really big. No matter, I washed them down with filtered water and within a couple of days I was feeling much better. That's when I learned the source of these magic pills.

I was talking with some family members, including

Stellita, and was thanking them for the medicine and commenting on how well it had worked. I said they must have really been powerful pills because they were gigantic. Stellita said that they were indeed powerful. Then she smiled and said they were actually horse pills and her friend the doctor was actually a veterinarian.

At first I was stunned then we all shared a good laugh. From that point forward, with good humor I must add, I always asked more questions when referred to a doctor.

The Ghost

At one point my father-in-law had purchased a beautiful black car that had once been a presidential limousine. I think it was a Packard, but no matter, it was a classic and he loved that car. Given the large physical size of the car and small frame of my father-in-law it was a sight to see him drive it, but he did it well. He actually had to look through the steering wheel to see the road.

One night he had worked very late at his shop and had also had a few drinks before heading home. (This was, of course, long before strict drinking and driving laws.) Upon pulling up in the driveway he switched off the engine and sat there. In an exhausted state he dozed off. As he slumped behind the steering wheel he was barely visible. His eyeglasses slid down his nose, affecting what he could clearly see.

My mother-in-law had heard the car pull up and after

a period of time became concerned when her husband failed to appear. She got out of bed and pulled a white blanket over her heard to ward off the chill of night air and headed toward the driveway. As she approached the car she saw a form huddled in the seat. She knocked on the window. My father-in-law was roused out of his brief nap and looked up.

Later he would say that he saw a ghost-like figure gliding toward the car. In his panic he jumped from the driver's side of the car to the passenger seat and drew his knees up towards his chest. His eye glasses slipped even further down his nose. He let out a loud startled yell as the figure peered in the window at him. This in turn startled my mother-in-law and she started screaming. So there they were, both staring and screaming. She turned and fled back into the house.

After things calmed down they shared a laugh, but at the time, he swore he had seen a ghost. She said what really scared her was that she heard the shocked shriek and the fact that he was mostly hidden hunched down in the seat. I don't do this story justice, but the way they told it, I never tired of hearing it. And no matter how often I heard it I would laugh so hard it would bring tears to my eyes.

The Cane Field

In 1980, during a family visit to Bogota, we decided to visit my wife's sister Mary and her family in Pasto. Other family members also expressed a desire to go,

A snapshot at my eldest bother-in-law Hector's farm in Sylvania circa 1986. Left to right, my sister-in-law Mary; the author; Maria Angelica, a niece; her husband; Hector; and a niece and nephew, Esperanza and her brother Juan Manual.

but wanted to drive. Since my wife was several months pregnant with our daughter Natalie and didn't want to sit through a 18 plus hours long road trip, we decided she would fly and I would drive with my mother-in-law and two of my sisters-in-law, Esperancita and Margarita.

We planned to go in Esperancita's car. Before I go any further, you have to understand that for years we have teased her about her driving habits, which include turning completely around while driving so she can make eye contact with a person she is talking to in the backseat. In addition to being a delightful person, I would be remiss if I also didn't note that Esperanza has great karma, leads a charmed life, and is a very smart and successful business woman.

The trip was set and a few days later we headed out in a Renault 4, which was a popular small four seater during that time. In essence, it was a clown car, cramped and made even worse since the manual gearshift extended horizontally out from the dashboard between the driver and the front passenger.

It was midday by the time we left and Esperancita was driving. I quickly discovered that the ladies liked to stop at virtually every pueblo to buy snacks and specialty foods of the particular areas we passed through. Consequently, progress was slow and it promised to be a very long trip, especially since we planned to drive the 1000 kilometers straight through.

It was a little before dark when I glanced over and

noticed that the little ammeter on the dashboard was indicating minus instead of plus, which meant the battery was discharging. Admittedly I am no mechanic and my knowledge of cars is limited, but I was reasonably certain that it was caused by either a broken belt to turn the generator or the generator itself was bad. I pointed this out to Esperancita, but she merely waved me off with her upbeat attitude and assured me that everything was just fine. She said this was Colombia and things were the way things were and worked the way they worked. She was so convincing, I thought maybe I was wrong, but it still bothered me.

If I was right, I wondered how long the battery would last, but finally shrugged it off. As it got dark, though, and we switched on the headlights, the meter pointed even lower. Again I said something was wrong. About the time we were having this conversation on a dark lonely stretch of road, of course, the engine died for lack of electricity to the sparkplugs. We coasted to a stop and the ever optimistic Esperancita announced that it was a small problem and we would quickly figure out how to deal with it. I checked the engine and discovered a broken fan belt.

Esperancita flagged down a passing truck and the driver kindly gave us a lift to a gas station at the edge of the next town a few kilometers down the road. They did not have our part, but a guy at the station said a cousin had an auto parts store in town and for a nominal fee he would drive us there. He did so, except that when we arrived, the store was closed for the night since it was getting late by this time. The man assured us, however, that this was no problem and we headed to the cousin's house where we roused the poor man out of his bed.

He was gracious and after he dressed we went back to his store where we finally got the right part. The pair then kindly offered to drive us back to the disabled vehicle, which we gratefully accepted. They dropped us off and left. I then asked Esperancita if she had a tool kit, which she didn't. I had incorrectly assumed that most Colombian vehicles carried at least some basic tools, given the nature of the roads and the often long distances at that time between shops or gas stations.

Great, I thought. I now have a fan belt, but no tools, not even a pair of pliers or an adjustable wrench. So we stood in the dark. I must say, Esperancita and the others were unflappable and confident that this would all somehow work out. For my part, I was a little frustrated and anxious. It turned out they were right.

Another truck stopped to aid us and the driver quickly installed the belt. Then we put the little car in gear and he and I pushed it a few feet as Esperancita popped the clutch and it started right up. We were back in business and I noted with satisfaction that the ammeter indicated that the generator was charging the depleted battery. Music blaring, off we went merrily into the night.

As we drove up the curvy road toward la linea, where the mountains soar to over 12,000 feet, I could tell she was tired and offered to drive. She declined at first, but finally allowed me behind the wheel and we continued on the two-lane road headed up the big central range of the Andes. After driving for a while traffic came to an abrupt standstill. We found ourselves on a very steep incline on a curve with a line of cars stretching up the mountain, taillights for as far as we could see. We learned that it was the result of an accident.

Finally, traffic started moving. By this time my companions had the radio cranked up to a music station and were happily chatting with each other. The music was so loud I couldn't hear the engine at all. Anyone who has ever driven a stick shift car and started from a stop on a hill will know what I'm talking about. I set the brake, gunned the little engine, which I couldn't hear, and popped the clutch. It stalled, but every time I would turn down the radio a little one of them would crank it back up. We kept rolling backwards toward the car behind us, but finally got going. I was sweating in the cool air.

By the time we had crested the mountain I was tense and tired from gripping the wheel in my efforts to drive the intimidating road in darkness and heavy traffic. So, Esperancita and I again traded places. We were headed down the other side towards the vast coastal lowlands where we would bypass the city of Cali.

Sometime during the night, even in my cramped seat, I nodded off into an uneasy sleep. Right before dawn, though, I was abruptly awoken by a loud and incessant thumping sound. As my eyes snapped open I was momentarily confused as the headlights illuminated a sea of large green stalks surrounding us. Then it hit me. We were in the middle of a sugar cane field.

By the light of the dashboard Esperanza and I exchanged glances and then burst out laughing. I insisted I would drive and got little argument from her. As I maneuvered the Renault back through the mowed down swath of cane, I was amazed how far off the road we were. God was I happy we hadn't been on top of that mountain.

Somewhat sheepishly Esperanza said she must have dozed off and set us thumping through the big cane field as we whacked down stalks. I must say, though, she was unbelievably unflustered, finding humor in what had happened. Proving once again that all is well that ends well. We continued across the lowlands and back up into the mountains, passing Popayan and finally reaching Pasto without further incident. (Instead of 18 hours, it took 25.)

Was that a Tire That Just Passed Us?

Ironically, it was with Esperanza's daughter, Esperanza chiquita that I would share another memorable road trip years later. I had known her since she was a small child. So when we visited her in Barranquilla, it was always so amazing to see her as a beautiful young mother and business woman.

We stayed a few days at her home. She then invited

us to drive to Santa Marta, a beautiful beach town, and after that to spend a few days in Cartagena, which had long been one of my favorite cities. During our drive I noticed that one of the tires was making a noise and mentioned it to her. She said she had told her father. At the time my brother-in-law, Noel, manufactured radiators and had large mechanical shops in several cities. He told her it was nothing and not to worry about it. Still I could tell it bothered her and it certainly bothered me.

It was a sunny day and we were on a nice stretch of road outside Cartagena. She was driving. I was in the passenger seat and my wife behind us. We were all chatting when we heard a loud banging noise. I glanced over just as the rear tire on the driver's side went rolling by, literally zooming past the car. Almost immediately the rear axle hit the pavement and sparks started to fly.

She skillfully wrestled the car to a stop on the side of the road. Everyone was fine. We found a telephone and called a tow truck, which turned out to be a big jeep. That's when the truly terrifying ride started.

A bracket with chains was welded to the cabin of our unconventional tow truck. I watched as the driver placed a thick wooden post across the back of our disabled car, hooked the chains under the frame and over the beam, and hoisted the vehicle up. The end result was that it was now suspended with the front of the car facing backwards. Since there was only room for Esperanza chiquita to ride in the truck, my wife and I climbed into the front seat of the broken car. We strapped ourselves in to keep from sliding off the seat because of the incline.

Night had settled in around us and everything seemed just fine. We had been rescued. As soon as we started moving, though, I noticed that the suspended car tended to swing from side to side. The arc became even wider as we gathered speed and the driver negotiated the twists and turns in the road. Since we were facing backwards, we could see other cars zoom towards us with blinding lights, then pass at the last second as we swung at the end of the chain like fish on a pole.

Our adrenaline was definitely in overdrive as we swayed helplessly, often dangerously, into the oncoming traffic lane. It was with great relief that we arrived back at the house and were deposited into the driveway. As we climbed out of the car we felt like sailors stepping onto the comforting feel of solid ground after a long sea voyage.

Even now, hearing my wife describe the experience conjures up an almost cartoon-like image of us dangling behind the big Jeep, a bit terrified and unable to communicate with those up front. Although at the time it was very unsettling, the thought of it now makes us all laugh.

So Many Fond Memories

My feelings of love and respect for the family are universal and unconditional, but spending more time with some than others has naturally caused a particular fondness for certain relatives. One such member was the husband of Dorita, my wife's youngest sister. Alvaro was always full of support, good cheer, and a great joker.

From the early days, my father-in-law would always talk very loudly to me. For some reason he thought that this would make Spanish more understandable to my gringo ear. When he would gesture and tell me things in this manner, Alvaro would laugh and say, "Luis, he doesn't understand everything in Spanish. He's not deaf." With his self-deprecating humor my father-in-law would laugh.

Alvaro was the epitome of integrity. His word and handshake were worth any ten signed contracts. He loved to play cards with me. I should mention that cards are not really my thing and they were often games with nuances that I didn't fully understand. Consequently, he would generally win big. Knowing his extraordinarily honest disposition, I would then good naturedly accuse him of cheating. I loved to watch him protest vigorously as I kept chiding him. It was almost worth losing to see his reaction.

Over the years he and Dorita built a successful snack food business from a home operation to a large, sophisticated factory with national distribution and sales. They eventually sold out to a larger conglomerate and set about to enjoy life without the grind of running a major manufacturing operation. His sudden passing was a blow to everyone. His memory, though, is vividly etched in my mind because over the thirty plus years we hung out together, I can't even begin to describe how much he made me laugh. To this day his grown son and three daughters are like my own. They are part of a long list of nieces and nephews that number in the dozens.

To be sure, like all families, we have suffered other losses. Hector, another brother-in-law is also gone, but up to the last day I looked forward to spending time with him. I loved his sense of humor and there was no such thing as a boring conversation with him. At the end, we reminisced about such things as our games of rana or zapo, which is a typical Colombian game featuring a brass frog. You throw metal disks and try to score by hitting the slot in the frog's mouth or slots in the wooden box that it's mounted on. We would sometimes frequent small bars or tiendas and drink beer, choose sides with other family members and have epic battles between my US team and his national team. I usually lost, but it was great fun.

Many of these games took place as we traveled to his finquita. This is a little farm and if you spend any time in Colombia you soon realize that a great many people who live in the city maintain modest places in the country to get away or to host family gatherings.

One of my oldest sisters-in-law also died. Margarita was a talented artist and she lives on through her paintings and her wonderful children. The family is still large and growing and the oldest sister, Mary, is now the person we look up to. Smart, funny, and strong willed there is never a dull moment around her. Not surprising, I look forward to my trips south and spending time with her and my brother-in-law Eudoro.

As I mentioned early in this book, Mary and Eudoro are the primary reason we ended up in Pasto in 1984. At that time he was an executive with the Banco Cafetero (the coffee grower's bank) and he helped us acclimate to our new city. This included offering us the hospitality of his home for many weeks while we looked for a house to lease.

Two of my wife's sisters, Leticia and Cocho, live in the States so I have been fortunate enough to spend more time with them than I have with those in Colombia. Both are great cooks and through the years their fabulous and authentic Colombian dishes have been something to be savored. Their fiestas have served to remind all of us that life is meant to be shared with the warmth of family, with a healthy measure of laughter and dancing thrown in to the mix.

It is not my intent to unduly single out certain members of the family, because all my brothers-in-law and sisters-in-law—Mary, Margarita, Stellita, Esperancita, Leticia, Cocho, Dorita, Luis Eduardo, and Hector—have played a special part in my life and I am richer for it. I have too many nieces and nephews to mention, but they are also special to me. All of these wonderful individuals were the human infrastructure that enabled me to live and work in the country. They are also the reason I always look forward to visiting.

I truly believe they are representative of the Latin family, which forms the incomparable backbone of the remarkable country that is Colombia. It is my belief that the vibrancy and closeness of such families is what makes Colombia such a special place. It's comparable to the families in the US in the early and mid-20th century before they started to shrink in size and scatter geographically.

EPILOG
COLOMBIA, CENTRAL TO THE FUTURE

The look at the past in this book would not be complete without at least a glimpse into the future based on how yesterday and today are blending to shape tomorrow.

Like most countries, Colombia's fortunes have always reflected the man at the top. When there has been an effective president, security has increased and the economy has tended to prosper. During the 1980s, for example, under what I consider to be the disastrous administration of President Belisario Betancur, the guerrillas increased their power, the cocaine cartels flourished, and the stability and security of the country suffered. I remember clearly that his favorite words were, "la paz, la paz." (the peace, the peace) Indeed, he talked continually about peace. But other than repeating his favorite phrase and conducting largely non-productive peace talks with the guerrillas, in my opinion he accomplished little.

He was followed by several other presidents who failed to deal effectively with the armed insurgence and the drug cartels. Finally, under President Andres Pastrana, from 1998 to 2002, the effectiveness of the chief executive reached a low point. Pastrana believed that by accommodating the guerrillas he could resolve the decades old problem. He went so far as to give them a "free zone" roughly the size of Switzerland in the heart of Colombia. It was to be a safe haven for them while peace talks were conducted. This policy of appeasement didn't work. Much was said, but little was accomplished, except for the guerrillas getting a free ride for several years.

That all changed with the election of Alvaro Uribe, who was inaugurated president in August of 2002. He was elected with a strong electoral mandate to fulfill his pledge to enhance the state's authority and guarantee security. Although he promised to search for a negotiated settlement to the long standing armed conflict with insurgent groups (such as the ELN, FARC, and M-19, as well as the conservative paramilitary AUC), it was obvious from the start that he intended to be tough and no nonsense. Accordingly, he conditioned his promise to talk with the guerrilla groups on implementation of a ceasefire and complete suspension of hostilities. Absent that, he stated his intention to unleash the full power of Colombian military forces on the insurgents.

The FARC, sensing that the game was about to change, mounted a mortar attack in the center of

Bogota by attempting to shell the Casa Nariño during Uribe's inauguration ceremony. Undaunted, Uribe showed his grit by pressing on. He was so successful in his campaign against the rebels that the Colombian National Congress and courts changed the country's constitution restricting presidents to one term. This enabled him to run for a second consecutive term. By the time he left office in 2010 he was one of Colombia's longest serving presidents. He was succeeded by Juan Manuel Santos, his former defense minister.

Although this book is about a gringo's Colombian journey and not Colombian politics per se, I would be remiss if I didn't point out that while Uribe is admired by many, he was (and still is) fiercely criticized by some, especially on the liberal side of the political spectrum. Many claim that in dramatically enhancing the country's security he trampled on human and civil rights and aligned himself with right wing paramilitary groups. I don't pretend to know with any certainty what are absolute facts, lies, or myths. All I can say is that in talking to my family and friends and from personal experience, I have not found that to be the case. I clearly remember the wild west atmosphere of Colombia during the 1980s and saw the dramatic changes that had occurred by the mid-2000s under his leadership.

In addition, over the years many journalists and political rivals have sought to link him to the drug mafia. Again, I have no way of knowing what, if any, of these allegations are true. Those who tend to believe conspiracy theories certainly have a lot of material to work with. I have personally found most of it, though, to be coincidental at best. They point, for example, to some photos of Uribe at parties or gatherings where some mafia members were present. I have looked at many of these pictures and have not found them to be conclusive of anything. As a politician from Medellin it was inevitable that such material would surface. After all, politicians attend a lot of functions and social events. One such photo, for instance, shows him in the same room at a social function as Pablo Escobar. Certainly interesting until you remember that there was a period when Escobar was in Congress.

Plus, a helicopter found during the raid on Tranquilandia was said to be owned by Uribe's father. Papers, though, appear to show that the helicopter was sold before the drug raid. In addition, his father was murdered by the FARC who by that time were working with the drug cartels.

So, many of the allegations make little sense to me. To my knowledge no one has found a "smoking gun" to lend much credence to the myriad of allegations and conspiracies associated with Uribe. I simply don't know and have no way of judging the man except by his remarkably successful record in restoring the country's stability and security, a time during which the economy prospered.

He brought security to a level that one can now drive safely throughout the country without fear of being kidnapped. This has tended to attract investors and the economy is functioning smoothly, despite the current global economic woes.

The tough independent conservative was starkly different than his predecessors and he appears to have been the right man for the job at the right time. I believe he set the tone for the current Colombian administration, ensuring that the country remains the staunchest US ally in South America. This relationship is essential to the US in an emerging sea of political turmoil, for example, Hugo Chavez in Venezuela, Evo Morales in Bolivia, and Rafael Correa in Ecuador. Morales is an avowed socialist. In fact, his political party name is Movement for Socialism and he has forged strong ties with fellow socialist Chavez and communists Raul and Fidel Castro in Cuba. Left leaning Correa is also a disciple of Chavez.

Few would argue that Colombia has not been dramatically affected by the drug mafia or its propensity for violent clashes between the government and guerrillas. Yet, over the years it has become increasingly clear to me that Colombia plays not only a key role to the US and the hemisphere because of its strategic location, but also because of its extraordinary ability to sustain democracy and avoid military coups. In general, no matter if a liberal or conservative occupies Casa Nariño, they seem to have the uncanny ability to navigate the middle of the political road and avoid extremism. In essence, I believe Colombia is the keystone to regional security.

Based on my travels, work, and experiences in the region, here's a brief look at what I believe is ultimately at stake not just for Colombia and South America, but for the US as well. Based on this, I predict that at some point in the future, events will compel the US to become involved in South America at a level we have never seen. The stakes will be as high as those we currently have in the Middle East.

Consider, for example, Hugo Chavez. Based on his emerging ties with Iran, the Venezuelan leader has expressed his intent to pursue nuclear weapons. I have no doubt that if he manages to survive and stay in power he will do that. If successful, it would change politics in the Americas in unimaginable ways, making our true allies, like Colombia, paramount to our national well-being. Or perhaps, as I've written elsewhere, the land to our south could become a second 9-11 in the ongoing war on terrorism.

Oil and Money—the Twin Towers of the Americas[10]

Attacking a country other than the US could hurt America more than a direct assault like 9-11, resulting in a devastating domino effect that would topple a number of economies throughout the Americas.

---

10   Adapted from "The Americas—A Ticking Terrorist Time Bomb," by Michael F. Kastre, translated into Spanish and published in Imagin Washington magazine, Spring 2004.

What makes the Americas so vulnerable and attractive to terrorists are the very interdependencies that unite the region. From the US and Uruguay to Colombia, Canada, and Chile, the futures of all the countries of the Americas are integral to each other. And, the key sectors of petroleum and finance are the most vulnerable elements.

Oil and banking are like the former twin towers. These targets have the potential to make 9-11 look like a firecracker in comparison. Perhaps not in the total number of human casualties, but in the potentially devastating impact on the collective economies of the Americas. With the heavy US dependence on oil from Mexico and Venezuela and the billions in trade and loans among the countries, a single terrorist act in South America could create an energy crisis unprecedented in nature or cause banks to fail in North America and regional economies to crumble to the south.

That's because in recent years, Venezuela has consistently ranked as one of the top sources of US oil suppliers, along with Mexico, Canada, and Saudi Arabia. The US now depends on Mexican and Venezuelan petroleum for roughly 25 percent of its oil needs. Those countries in turn depend upon that revenue to ensure the stability of their own economies. In Venezuela, for instance, the petroleum industry accounts for more that 75 percent of the country's total export revenues, over half the government's revenues, and over one-third of its Gross Domestic Product (GDP).

That is unlikely to change anytime soon because Venezuela has one of the Western Hemisphere's largest proven conventional oil reserves. It supplies major Caribbean refineries with significant quantities of crude oil, two of the largest being the Hovensa refinery on St. Croix and the Isla refinery on Curacao. About one-third of Venezuela's refined products are sold in the US. In addition, its state oil company, Petroleos de Venezuela S.A., operates several key pipelines needed to get oil out of fields like Maracaibo and the Zuata region of the Orinco belt for transport to Venezuela's northern coast.

To the North, Mexico, another major US supplier, has petroleum production facilities that also have a dramatic impact on both their state revenues and the operation of industry and transportation in the US and elsewhere in the Americas.

Its Antonio M. Amor refinery, for example, produces high-octane gasoline, diesel, and aviation fuel.

It's not difficult to imagine the crippling economic impact if a commercial, charter, or private airplane were crashed into one of the Venezuelan or Mexican production or refinery facilities, causing their destruction or severe damage. A significant reduction in oil production or refined petroleum products could send an unprecedented shock wave with far-reaching implications through the entire combined economies of the Americas, including not just transportation, but manufacturing and financial sectors as well. (Not to mention an attack on the important Brazilian energy production sector.)

This vulnerability has increased over the past decade as Latin countries have struggled to balance financial and credit needs with their ability to expand their economies and infrastructures. In 2004, for example, the 23 countries of Latin America and the Caribbean owed over $500 billion in foreign debt. Today that number is approximately one trillion dollars. It's estimated that the Latin American debt represents over one-third of the GDP of the region, based on statistics from international financial institutions and the commercial banking sector.

These billions of dollars in debt are carried by organizations like the World Bank, the International Monetary Fund, large US banks, and financial institutions in Europe and Asia. For good reasons, many bankers and traders fear that any disruption of the economies of those countries would force a default on the debt and spark a devastating devaluation of the currencies. In effect, it would trigger a global financial fiasco that would spread like wildfire through the Americas from the Rio Grande River to the Tierra del Fuego and from Canada deep into the heart of the US. The current global economic meltdown has made the situation even more ominous.

By ignoring the seeds of terrorism that have been sown and failing to either understand or fully support key allies, like Colombia, the US is potentially setting itself up for unprecedented problems. After all, what happens in any one country will send strong shock waves to every corner of the Western Hemisphere because in the end, all people of the Americas are Americans.

Like many South American countries, Colombia is characterized by profound issues. Elements such as inequitable income and wealth distribution, a lack of equal opportunity, drugs, and rebels present significant challenges. Unlike many of its neighbors, though, Colombia is anchored by the underlying strength and character of its people and its remarkable achievement of maintaining the oldest functioning democracy in South America. Also, of all the Latin countries, they are the one who has consistently extended the hand of friendship and collaboration to the US. Something we have not always done in return.

Colombia has done this despite our often sharply critical attitude towards their role as a major supplier of illegal drugs to the US. They also have done this despite their belief that we have been hypocrites on many issues. That is, how we often tend to ignore that the demand for drugs in the US is what creates such an illicit trade. Yet, to their credit, they continue to stand with the US in a world where we are often criticized by other nations.

Much has changed, yet little has changed since I worked in Colombia. It remains a vibrant and exciting place. No matter what may happen politically in the future, I for one remain optimistic that it will somehow survive and thrive. After all, it has withstood myriad political upheavals and natural disasters for over 500 years. Given its history and the nature of its people, it is most likely to withstand whatever it faces for another five centuries.

Hopefully, along the way, the US will forge stronger ties and foster a better understanding with our best ally to the south. For far too long we have tended to ignore events and friends in our own neighborhood.

Moreover, Latinos are now the largest minority within the US population. Their culture and perspective are becoming more deeply ingrained into the American dream and experience. Accordingly, it would serve all of us well to better understand our neighbors and fellow citizens. In addition, paying more attention to our south may enable us to avert a bigger catastrophe in the future than 9-11. Toward that end, we would do well to remember that Colombia is the cornerstone and portal to an entire continent.

CPSIA information can be obtained at www.ICGtesting.com
Printed in the USA
LVOW07s0812250215

428295LV00005B/539/P